MASTERING
MEMORY

MASTERING MEMORY

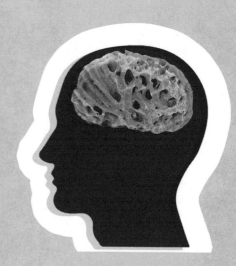

Techniques to
Turn Your Brain
from a Sieve
to a Sponge

CHESTER SANTOS *U.S. Memory Champion*

PUZZLE
WRIGHT
PRESS

New York

**PUZZLE
WRIGHT
PRESS**
New York

An Imprint of Sterling Publishing Co., Inc.
1166 Avenue of the Americas
New York, NY 10036

ISBN 978-1-4549-2080-9

Distributed in Canada by Sterling Publishing Co., Inc.
c/o Canadian Manda Group, 664 Annette Street
Toronto, Ontario M6S 2C8, Canada
Distributed in the United Kingdom by GMC Distribution Services
Castle Place, 166 High Street, Lewes, East Sussex BN7 1XU, England
Distributed in Australia by NewSouth Books
45 Beach Street, Coogee NSW 2034, Australia

For information about custom editions, special sales, and premium
and corporate purchases, please contact Sterling Special Sales
at 800-805-5489 or specialsales@sterlingpublishing.com.

Manufactured in Canada

4 6 8 10 9 7 5 3

sterlingpublishing.com

Cover design and endpapers by Ryan Thomann
Interior design by Sharon L.M. Jacobs
Picture Credits:
iStock: © angelinast: 79; © aristotoo: cover, vii (sponge); ©Azaze110: cover, vii
(profile); © benoitb: 15; © CSA Images/ B&W Engrave Ink Collection: 95;
© ilbusca: 57; © ivan-96: 87; © Man_Half-tube: 31; © nicoolay: xiv, 73;
© Pimonova: 23, 65

Shutterstock: © Canicula: 43; © Pim: 1

Contents

FOREWORD

COMPETITION is the hallmark of the business world.
If you are going to be a successful contestant in that world, you need a competitive advantage. Early in our lives, we measure our talents against those of others. With the help of feedback from schools and teachers, we settle in and work to develop, through training, our identified strengths so we can compete successfully and prosper. There is a dramatic "falloff" in our training after we stop formal education and we begin to accept where we are and what we have.

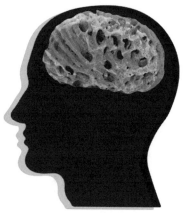

But not all of us stop or slow our skill training. The most successful people I know don't stop, but rather accelerate, their training. And these people succeed. Yes, they work harder, but they also work smarter. They are always looking for new edges and sharpening the edges they have. Their essential skills, such as reading, writing, listening, speaking, and remembering, just seem to get better. They excel because they don't take their skills for granted. They stay a step ahead. Reading and practicing the memory techniques and principles. in Chester's book will give you an edge and complement your other skills. How can I be so sure? Because Chester's training has dramatically "upped" my game.

I have been training with Chester since I met him in San Francisco in 2011. This training has helped me remember what happened in meetings without taking notes, and give talks, remarks, and speeches without having to read from scripts, notes, or slides. It has made it possible for me to remember telephone numbers, call-in codes, to-do lists, and countless other daily tasks I now take for granted. And I did all this in my fifties. At fifty-eight, my memory is better today than it was at any other age and is only improving.

While I can share countless examples of the practical impact of Chester's proven techniques, my favorite involves a sales meeting with a Fortune 100 company on behalf of my firm. Company officials summoned prospective suppliers, including representatives of my firm, to their headquarters for a final meeting. The purpose was to determine to which of us they would give their business. Five company representatives, one from each of the Fortune 100 company's business divisions, offered an overview of their needs. Along with the three other members of my team, I listened to each one. My colleagues kept looking up and down and scrambling to take notes. I listened intently, but, unbeknownst to anyone else, used this book's journey method to "record" key points and my solutions to the representatives' issues. This allowed me to engage each of the division leaders in a personal way. I smiled, nodded, and never lost eye contact. When they finished, I presented for our team. I recited all the issues and our proposed solutions. When I finished, all of their mouths were wide open. Their lead asked, "Did you write what we said on your hand?" I showed my hands and said, "No, I just listened. We listen to our customers." Of course, we won the contract.

Don't be complacent and accept your skills as they are. You can change them. You can improve your memory as you age. Memory is a beautiful edge because it affects so many other skills. Be a winner. Read Chester's book and train your mind to develop your edge to succeed.

Steven "Cash" Nickerson
President, PDS Tech Inc.
Author of *LISTENING AS A MARTIAL ART* and *STAGNATION*

EDITOR'S PREFACE

About two years ago I was at a luncheon in a large auditorium that was featuring a speech by a noted international memory expert. While casually nursing a glass of wine as I chatted with some friends before we took our places at the table, I noticed a gentleman roving around, greeting everyone in attendance.

The gent turned out to be the featured speaker, and as he took the microphone he asked everyone in the room to stand. There were almost a hundred of us. Then he asked us each to sit as he addressed each of us individually and called our name.

"Bill, Joe, Tony, Michael, Victor, Pedro, Ed . . ."

I watched, astonished, as he remembered every single attendee's name. Then, as part of his speech, he named a series of about twenty unrelated items: "monkey, kite, ribbon, house, rock, waterfall . . ." and then asked us to repeat them in order. Naturally, none of us could. It seemed impossible.

But with just a few of his tips, in a matter of minutes, we all recited the list in perfect order! It felt amazing to be able to do it. The entire audience was energized and inspired.

I soon discovered that our guest was Chester Santos, an internationally recognized memory champion and trainer who could perform feats of memorization that staggered the imagination. And, much to my surprise, when he was asked by many members of the audience for copies of his book for purchase, he replied that he had none.

I almost broke my neck rushing to the podium to introduce myself. As a writer, I recognized that this man had an important message that could help millions of people if it were in book form. I offered my assistance and we made a date to meet for lunch.

It turned out that Chester was in worldwide demand as a public speaker and memory expert. He has given speeches and performed amazing memory demonstrations in dozens of countries. In fact, Chester has been featured on just about every major-market TV news program and in every major metropolitan newspaper and magazine.

I helped Chester bring this book into the world because I believe the information contained in *Mastering Memory* will change the reader's life forever.

Edmond G. Addeo
Mill Valley, California

INTRODUCTION

We are living in the age of Google, GPS, Wikipedia, smartphones, and other apps and electronic devices. What they help us to do in our daily lives is incredible. However, we need to be wary of letting them remember everything for us. People use their memory less now than perhaps at any other time in history, and this is only getting worse.

Because it's so easy nowadays to look up information that you might need, why should you concern yourself with being able to remember things? Here are some points to consider:

1. The "use it or lose it" principle. Put simply, if you don't use your memory now, you may eventually lose it. Consider these examples:

- Most people find their memory to be sharpest during their school years, because that's when they use it the most. How is your memory now, compared to when you were in school?

- Before the days of cell phones, people were able to remember the phone numbers of friends and family members. Committing important numbers to memory was not a problem. If you're of a certain age, ask yourself: How many phone numbers can you remember today, compared to before the advent of the cell phone?

- London taxi drivers are famous for their amazing memory-based navigational abilities. So much so that, according to a study published in *Scientific American* in 2011, researchers studied their brains and verified that they had larger-than-average memory centers. When the GPS is down, how well do other taxi drivers navigate these days?

The "*use it or lose it*" principle also applies to your overall brain health. Alzheimer's disease, dementia, and Parkinson's disease are more common today because we're living longer. Doctors around the world are now recommending brain exercise programs in addition to physical exercise routines. Memory training is wonderful exercise for your brain and can help keep you sharp throughout your life, especially in your later years.

2. Demonstration of expertise. Memory is fundamental to learning, and learning leads to knowledge. Without memory there is no knowledge, and without knowledge you cannot demonstrate your expertise. Let's say, for example, you consult with two attorneys. One is always looking everything up. The other is incredibly knowledgeable and can cite laws relevant to your case from memory. Which attorney are you more likely to hire? Or imagine that you interview two real estate agents. One agent has memorized key information about many different properties on the market and is able to talk about them all—whether she runs into a potential client at the grocery store, tennis club, or a networking event. The other agent has a poor memory. When running into potential clients, he often has to offer to get back to them later, and then may subsequently forget to follow up. Which agent would you rather list with?

This point is important not only for attorneys and real estate agents, but also for financial advisers, business consultants, and more. By demonstrating your expertise through knowledge, you will be perceived as much more of an *expert* in your particular field. I always try to hire an expert over a novice or an apprentice.

3. Perception. There is a common perception that someone with a razor-sharp memory is intelligent. (Whether or not that's truly the case is up for debate.) We are drawn to intelligence and want to interact with intelligent people in business, in school, and in social settings.

4. Presentation skills. I've been fortunate to speak at conferences and corporate events with people who are world-renowned experts in their fields. Sadly, some of these speakers failed to capture the audience's attention, because they spent their entire speech reading through their PowerPoint slides, thus putting the audience to sleep. Having a great memory can help you with presentations, because you can memorize at least the key points of your speech. This applies to almost any occupation, and can make you a much more effective speaker, allowing you to better interact with and engage your audience.

5. Building rapport. Remembering names helps you to build rapport with people. Think about it and you'll quickly realize that the most popular people you know tend to be very good with names. Remembering names can help to develop relationships; forgetting them can be detrimental.

The above considerations are just a small sampling of the reasons it's important to have a good memory, even in today's society. The ability to quickly and easily remember anything you want can serve as a "superpower," giving you a huge advantage in multiple areas of your life. Imagine yourself with unlimited mental access to important facts and figures, names, presentations, languages, and more. I want you to realize and believe that this is well within your reach.

I've spoken all over the world, appeared in newspapers and magazines, and been interviewed on radio, television, and film. Some of the feats of memory that I've performed over the years have been called "extraordinary" and "mind-blowing." I have managed to perfectly memorize hundreds of names, playing cards, random digits, and more in a matter of minutes. Some larger-scale feats have included memorization of all Kentucky Derby results since the race's inception in 1875, not only including the names of the horses, but also their jockeys, and over four thousand pieces of data about the U.S. Congress that I demonstrated in front of a large audience in New York City.

I mention all this not to try to impress you, but rather to *impress upon you* the fact that these things are all possible with training. Everything I've been able to do is the result of *training* and *practice*. You can do it, too!

Your brain is remarkable and you are capable of doing much more with it than you might think is possible. With this book, I will help you unlock more of your brain's full potential. If you take the time to read through each chapter and complete the exercises, and *practice*, you will soon be amazing your colleagues, family members, and friends with your superpowered memory!

Before we get started, I want to quickly emphasize that this is not a book about the broad topic of human memory. There are many aspects of memory that I will not touch on in this book. This book's primary aim is to help you develop valuable memory *skills* that you can apply throughout your life.

This is also not a *comprehensive* book on memory training. I'm familiar with many memory techniques that I purposely chose not to include in this book. I've decided to spotlight only those techniques, based on my decades' worth of experience teaching memory skills, that I feel will be of most use, and of greatest interest, to the general population. This book will be valuable for students, teachers, executives, entrepreneurs, other professionals, and anyone else who would like to reap the benefits of an improved memory and a sharper mind.

I'm incredibly excited to be your guide along this journey toward acquiring skills that will benefit you for a lifetime. I wish I could see the look on your face as you experience yourself doing amazing things with your memory. Although I can't be there in person, I hope you'll feel free to share your experiences with me on Twitter (@ChesterJSantos).

Cheers to your continued success!

Chester Santos
"The International Man of Memory"

THE FUNDAMENTAL RULES APPLY

You are about to learn a number of techniques that will quickly improve your ability to remember whatever you want to. Over time, these techniques will result in improved memory, concentration, imagination, creativity, and visualization ability. Believe it or not, this process is also going to be a lot of fun! As you complete the exercises in this first chapter and throughout the book, I'd like you to approach them as entertaining challenges in flexing your imagination, rather than difficult memory exercises. This shift in your mind-set when it comes to committing things to memory is going to make a huge difference in your recall ability. If you focus on just relaxing and having fun while reading through my examples and explanations, you will soon be remembering more than you ever thought possible.

I'm about to help you unlock the extraordinary power of your mind!

GET A VISUAL

First, we are going to work on using your imagination. The power of your imagination is directly related to your ability to remember. This will become clearer to you as we progress through your memory training. I'm about to describe an interesting scenario to you; your task for now is simply to do your best to **visualize** it. See it in your mind to the best of your ability. I want to stress here that the imagery does not need to be crystal clear. Just picture everything as best you can.

Imagine that you walk into your current residence and you see Donald Trump and Hillary Clinton. Experience this as vividly as possible, as if it were actually happening—Donald Trump and Hillary Clinton in your very own living room! They look as if they are about to engage in a debate. Try to feel some of the shock and bewilderment that you would if you actually came home to see this. Although what you're witnessing has you very confused, you decide to just hang back and observe, rather than asking any questions. Trump and Clinton are glaring at each other. Suddenly, Trump reaches behind his podium and he pulls out a pie. He then throws it at Clinton and—**splat!**—hits her right in her face! She is not amused in the least, and now she pulls out a pie from behind her podium as well. She throws it at Trump and covers his face in pie to match hers.

What presumably started off as a debate has at this point turned into a full-blown pie fight. The politicians are continuously throwing pies at each other. Picture this happening as best you can and be sure to have fun with it. If you're smiling or giggling to yourself, it's a great sign that you're in the right mind-set for this exercise. At this point you're experiencing imagery in your mind. Next, try to involve even more senses as you witness this funny scenario happening in your mind's eye. In addition to **seeing** the fight, you can now **hear** it happening as well. Spend a few seconds focusing on imagining the sound. Next, you start to *smell* the pies—a sharp, pungent aroma. You now walk over to one of the podiums and scoop up some of the pie. Really experience the *feeling* of the pie in your hands. Finally, taste some of the pie and focus on imagining the flavor in your mouth. What can you taste?

Wasn't that exercise fun and easy to do? Well, I have great news for you. If you were able to complete that exercise, you are absolutely capable of quickly and easily remembering just about anything at all. Without realizing it, by completing that exercise with Trump and Clinton, you touched on the three main principles for memory improvement:

1. Visualization: Turn whatever you'd like to commit to memory into a simple image or series of images that you can easily visualize and see in your mind.

2. Additional Senses: Beyond visualization, involve as many additional senses as possible. As you involve more senses when trying to commit information to memory, you are activating more areas of your brain and building more connections in your mind to the information, making it much easier to retrieve when you need it later on.

3. Creativity: Use your creativity and imagination to make what you are seeing and experiencing in your mind as unusual as possible. This helps you tap into the psychological aspect to human memory. Without putting forth much effort at all, we can more easily remember things that catch us by surprise and that are out of the ordinary. If, at this very moment, an elephant were to crash into the room that you're in and spray water on you with its trunk as you're reading this book, you'd likely remember it for the rest of your life without even trying!

Let's now apply what you learned from the exercise with the politicians to easily memorize a random list of words.

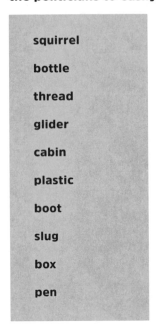

squirrel

bottle

thread

glider

cabin

plastic

boot

slug

box

pen

The random word list on the left can easily be memorized if you relax and use your imagination. Imagine that you see a little **squirrel** dancing around. Picture him clearly in your mind. Not only can you see the squirrel, but you can also hear him making strange noises. His antics amuse you. While you're watching the squirrel, all of a sudden he picks up a giant **bottle** and starts to dance with it. Visualize and experience this scenario in your mind as vividly as you can. Eventually, the weight of the bottle makes it fall. As it falls, a **thread** appears and becomes attached to the end of the bottle. You now walk up and feel the thread. Looking at the top of the thread, you see that it is tied to a **glider**. You reach up to try to touch the glider, but you can't quite reach it. The glider flies around and crashes into the side of a **cabin**. For some strange reason, this cabin is completely covered in **plastic**. You touch the plastic and, as you do, a **boot** magically appears and starts to walk all over the plastic, causing it to shift around. The boot smells very bad. You decide to investigate and look inside the boot. There you find an ugly **slug** crawling around. The slug approaches you, but then suddenly jumps out of the boot and into a **box**. This box is strange. It magically seals itself up. Then you notice a **pen** magically appear and begin to write on the box.

To recall the entire random word list, you now simply need to replay this funny and extraordinary story in your mind, starting with the squirrel. Each major object you encounter as you go through the story will give you the words: squirrel, bottle, thread, glider, cabin, plastic, boot, slug, box, pen. If you get stuck, just reread the story. As I keep stressing, do your best to relax and have fun with what you are seeing and experiencing in your mind. If you're relaxed, having a good time, and vividly experiencing the *story*, nearly instant recall of what you're trying to remember will be the natural result. You've just learned your first memory technique— it's called the *story method*. The story method is an effective and powerful technique that is also versatile.

Let's extend the list and see how it works:

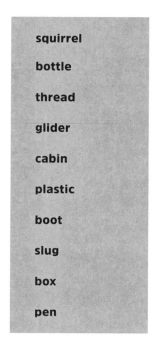

squirrel
bottle
thread
glider
cabin
plastic
boot
slug
box
pen

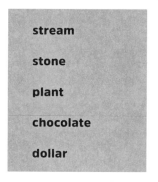

stream
stone
plant
chocolate
dollar

Once the pen finishes writing on the box, it jumps into a roaring **stream**. You notice this stream crashes against a **stone**; the stone crashes into a **plant**, which has **chocolate** growing from it instead of leaves. A giant **dollar** bill shoots out of each piece of chocolate. Review the extended story once more and then effortlessly recall all fifteen words in order.

You'll find that it's easy to do this both forward and backward! And if you repeat this story tonight before you go to sleep, or first thing in the morning when you wake up, I'll bet you'll remember it for months to come—maybe even forever!

The story method helps you to remember information while also exercising your creativity. This particular memory technique primarily activates the right side of the brain, which is known to deal with creativity and imagination. It's an easy technique to use and works well in conjunction with more advanced techniques that I'll introduce you to later on in the book. As you continue practicing the story method, over time you'll be able to create imagery in your mind more quickly and experience it more vividly.

TIP This book will help you develop your *semantic* memory; that is, your recall of facts, figures, names, presentations, vocabulary, and so on. In the TV show *Taxi,* Marilu Henner's character had a superior *episodic* memory, which is autobiographical in nature and not covered in this book. She could remember what she ate for breakfast twenty years ago, but she didn't have an exceptional ability to remember new facts, figures, or vocabulary.

BODY OF MEMORY

You're next going to learn how to use both the left and right sides of your brain at the same time when committing information to memory. The left side of your brain is known to deal with order and logic, which includes sequencing. You'll involve this side of your brain when trying to memorize something by first learning a list of locations in a logical order or sequence that makes sense to you. Once you know the list of locations in order, you can then use your creativity and imagination to come up with vivid imagery that will remind you in some way of what you're trying to remember. You can then mentally link the imagery to the locations. For recall, it just becomes a matter of taking a mental stroll back through the locations. As you do this, the images you see will remind you of what you committed to memory. I realize that this may sound a bit complicated at first. However, this is actually easy for *anyone* to do.

The first step is to make sure to know the locations in order. This won't take much effort, because I want you to use a natural ordering of locations on your body, starting from the bottom and moving up to the top. Here are the locations, in order:

LOCATION #1: **your left foot**

LOCATION #2: **your right foot**

LOCATION #3: **your knees**

LOCATION #4: **your waist**

LOCATION #5: **your belly button**

LOCATION #6: **your chest**

LOCATION #7: **your neck**

LOCATION #8: **your mouth**

LOCATION #9: **your nose**

LOCATION #10: **the top of your head.**

Let's review: left foot, right foot, knees, waist, belly button, chest, neck, mouth, nose, top of your head. I recommend that you put additional focus on each body part by pointing at it or wiggling it as you get to it during your review of the locations. Before you move on to the next paragraph make sure that you can recite all the body locations both forward and backward.

Since you now know the body locations in the order I specified, you can actually use those locations to store new information. They will serve as mental filing cabinets. You'll see what I mean as I have you memorize the following word list in the box below.

orange

clock

suitcase

stick

truck

ball

bumblebee

ring

golf club

comb

To accomplish this task of word memory, you'll once again flex your creativity and imagination. Instead of one long story, however, you will come up with shorter stories happening at each location of your body. Things that I'm about to describe may seem ridiculous, painful, and even scary. However, I'm evoking these sensations for a reason. If you vividly experience what I describe, you won't be able to forget this list, even if you try! I'll once more stress that you should approach this activity as a fun exercise in creativity and imagination, rather than as a memorization task. That shift in mind-set is going to make a huge difference in your ability to remember things. Let's go!

Imagine that underneath your left foot is a large **orange**. You are rolling that orange around with your left foot. Really try to feel it under your foot. Now imagine that you begin to stomp on the orange and smash it. You smash it so hard that it begins to turn into orange juice. Try your best to experience this as if it were actually happening.

You notice a **clock** strapped to your right foot. The clock begins ticking loudly. It's ticking faster and faster, getting louder and louder. All of a sudden, the glass face of the clock shatters!

You look at your knees and see a giant **suitcase** attached to them. You reach down and push the button to open the suitcase and, when you do, water splashes all over your face as the suitcase opens.

All of a sudden, you feel a pain in the side of your waist, as if something is lodged there. You look and see a handle sticking out of your side. You pull on the handle and out slides a **stick.** Unbelievably, there was a stick lodged in your waist!

Now, you feel and hear rumbling coming from near your belly button. The rumbling is getting louder and louder. It begins to sound like an engine. Suddenly, a **truck** shoots out of your belly button! You can hear the truck's engine roaring and can see its tires spinning.

Ouch! Something has just hit you in the chest. You look and see that a **ball** is continuously hitting you there. You struggle to try to stop it, but you can't. The ball keeps hitting you in the chest and there is nothing you can do about it.

As if things couldn't get any worse, you see and hear a **bumblebee**, buzzing and circling around you. You are afraid that it might sting you, and then, without warning, it does sting you, right in the neck.

Now, you feel a pain coming from your mouth. Your tongue is stinging and you feel something attached to it. You pull on the object and discover that it's a **ring**! As you pull on the ring, it stretches your tongue.

On the tip of your nose a **golf club** teeters back and forth. With some effort, you're able to get your head into the correct position to perfectly balance the golf club on your nose.

You now feel a sudden urge to comb your hair. Luckily there seems to already be a **comb** stuck in it. You try to use the comb, but it starts to pull out some of your hair!

It should now be easy for you to recall the list of random words in order, by merely thinking of each part of your body in the sequence outlined above. When you think of your left foot, the orange should come to mind. Thinking of your right foot should bring to mind the clock; your knees, the suitcase; your waist, the stick; your belly button, the truck; your chest, the ball; your neck, the bumblebee; your mouth, the ring; your nose, the golf club; and the top of your head, the comb.

Go ahead and now recite all the words in order by mentally visiting each body location. Now try it backward. You should be able to recall every item on the list in the correct order, backward and forward.

You've just learned the *body method*. It is another powerful and easy-to-use technique for improving your ability to remember. It is also extensible, but with limits. Using other parts of your body will give you more filing cabinets. Feel free to use whatever body parts you'd like as long as you first learn them in a logical sequence. A downside to this technique is that you will eventually run out of body parts to use. However, even with this limitation, the body method is still a powerful and useful tool to add to your memory arsenal.

TIP Don't be afraid to show off! Have your friends and family members write down or call out random words, and impress them with your ability to quickly memorize them.

RHYME AND REASON

With the techniques covered in this chapter so far, if I were to ask you for the fifth item on a list, you would need to go through the first four items before being able to give me the fifth. The next technique I'll introduce will allow you to instantly tell me the *n*th item or piece of information on a list. It's called the *peg list*. There are many different types of peg lists, but probably the easiest one to learn is the number/rhyme peg list. With this particular list, each word on the list rhymes with its respective number. This list can be changed, but let's start with one that works very well, in the box below.

1. bun

2. shoe

3. tree

4. door

5. hive

6. sticks

7. heaven

8. plate

9. wine

10. hen

Take a few minutes to review this list. As you review it, it's important to visualize an image for each word. For example, for 1/bun, you should picture a bun and really try to see it as clearly as possible in your mind. Make sure that you know the list well before proceeding to the next paragraph.

Now that you know the number/rhyme peg list and can recite it, let's apply it to learning another random word list. This will be similar to what we did with the body list, except that instead of linking vivid imagery to locations on your body, you will link vivid imagery to each of the items on the peg list.

Below is the new random word list.

remote control

card

magazine

computer

cell phone

basket

torch

star

sand

melon

Once again, relax and have fun as we go through the crazy and interesting scenarios. Imagine that you pick up a **remote control** and start to stuff it into a bun. You then start to eat the remote control along with the bun! Next, imagine that you are walking around and feel something in your shoe. It's really irritating you, so you decide to take off your shoe and see what you find. You reach inside and are surprised to pull out a **card**. Looking out your window, you see an unusual tree. At its top, you see a large **magazine** that appears to be growing out of the tree. The pages of the magazine turn as the wind blows. You now see a door magically appear before you. Curiosity forces you to attempt to open it. Unfortunately, the door is locked by a security device—not just a keypad, but a whole **computer**.

You punch in a bunch of combinations. Finally, after hitting the ENTER key on the computer a final time, the door swings open. Now, you'd like to make a cell phone call, but your phone is trapped inside a beehive. Bumblebees buzz around the phone, guarding it and making you afraid to reach for it. You finally feel brave enough to make the attempt and, sure enough, you are stung as you grab your **cell phone** from inside the hive. Next you see sticks flying through the air, smashing into a huge **basket**. The sticks, which seem to come from nowhere, keep hitting the basket, until it is finally demolished.

Now visualize heaven, seeing it as clearly as possible in your mind. It's incredibly beautiful. Suddenly, a large **torch** is lowered from heaven. The torch burns hotter and brighter the lower it goes. Soon the flame from the torch becomes so hot that the heat begins to hurt you. Feeling hungry, you now go into your cupboard for a plate. The plate you take out is extraordinary. It has a **star** on it that twinkles like a real star. There is no logical explanation for how the star on the plate could twinkle like this. It must be magic! You now open a bottle of your favorite wine, but something is wrong. The bottle is filled with **sand**! Try to experience the disappointment of being unable to drink your favorite wine, and imagine feeling the sand as it pours out of the bottle. Now I want you to picture seeing a giant hen. This hen is clucking loudly and pecking at a **melon**. You didn't know that hens ate melons, but this hen seems to be thoroughly enjoying it. As it pecks the melon, pieces of the fruit splatter all over the place.

Review all the scenarios described here before continuing to the next paragraph.

It should now be fairly easy to recall the list of random words by thinking of each item in the number/rhyme peg list. Also, you can now name the fifth random word in the list without having to go through the first four words. If I ask you to name the fifth word, *hive* should come to your mind, which in turn should make you think of *cell phone*. If I ask you to name the seventh word, *heaven* should come to mind and thus remind you of *torch*.

Go ahead and recite the entire random word list, starting with *remote control*. Now, do it backward! You've just added another powerful memory technique to your arsenal, and this is only the beginning!

At this point, you've become familiar with some important memory improvement fundamentals. If you continue to consistently practice what you learned in this chapter, you will dramatically improve your memory over time. Your ability to remember will soon become a "superpower" that will give you an edge in many different areas of your life. This training will also serve as great overall exercise for your brain, helping to keep your brain healthy and sharp. And remember—and I'll nag you a lot on this—*practice*!

2

SPEAK LIKE CICERO

You are about to learn the most effective method ever created
for giving speeches and presentations from memory without any
notes. The core technique originated with the ancient Greeks. It
was known as the method of loci, with *loci* meaning "location."
Later in history, Roman orators used this method to give hours-
long speeches from memory. At one point, it was commonly
referred to as the "Roman room method," because the famous
Roman orator Cicero used this technique to give speeches.
According to Cicero, the method was discovered when an ancient
Greek poet named Simonides attended a banquet for nobles.
At one point Simonides stepped outside, and the banquet hall
suddenly collapsed, mangling the bodies of everyone inside.
Simonides was able to identify each person who had attended the
banquet by visualizing the hall and each person's seating position.

TAKE A JOURNEY

Nowadays, this technique is commonly called the "journey method." With the journey method, as with the body method in the previous chapter, we first learn a list of locations in a logical order and then link images to those locations to remind us of things we want to remember. The difference, however, is that, instead of using locations on your body, you use locations from your environment. This means you will never run out of locations to use.

You may wish to use locations with a personal meaning. I use locations from my current apartment, apartments I've lived in previously, friends' houses, houses I lived in growing up, schools I've attended, places I've been on vacation, places I frequent often, and so forth. With this incredibly powerful technique, if you think about it, you can literally come up with thousands of locations to use for storing information in your mind. The collection of locations that you decide to use can be referred to as a "journey." The number of locations you include in a specific journey can be any number you feel comfortable with and that best suits the needs of the memorization task at hand. In other words, one of your journeys may consist of twenty to twenty-five locations, whereas other journeys might consist of fifty locations or even more than a hundred. Think of the journey method as a mental filing system. You can organize and file the information in any way that makes the most sense to you.

When you apply the journey method to memorizing a speech or presentation, the number of locations on your journey should ideally match the total number of points you want to get across to your audience. In preparing to give any speech or presentation, I highly recommend that you first thoroughly research your topic and then create an outline based on your research. The points of your outline should contain all the topics and subtopics that you feel are most important to cover in your presentation. If your outline ends up having twelve points, then your journey should consist of twelve locations.

Next, you'll need to utilize all the principles you learned in chapter 1 to come up with imagery that will remind you in some way of your points; you will then link that imagery to the corresponding locations of your journey. Imagery that will make you remember the first point will go at the first location of your journey, imagery that will remind you of the second point will go at the second location of your journey, and so on. When implementing this step, be sure to employ the memory improvement principles of visualization, drawing on additional senses, and using your creativity and imagination so that what you are seeing and experiencing in your mind is crazy or bizarre. The images you've placed at the various locations should effectively remind you of the points that you need to communicate to your audience.

A PRESIDENTIAL EXAMPLE

Let's go over how you would memorize a sample presentation to further clarify how this all works. Below is an outline for a short talk about the historic 2008 presidential election between Senators Barack Obama and John McCain, as it might have been given in the months before the election.

I. Obama or McCain: Who will win?

II. Democrats say that McCain can't win.

A. The Republican brand is shot due to George W. Bush, so the Republican candidate cannot win.

B. If McCain were to win, it would represent a third term for George W. Bush, and voters would never allow that.

C. McCain is too old. He would be the oldest president ever to hold office.

III. Republicans say that Obama can't win.

A. Obama was losing ground by the end of the Democratic nomination race, evidenced by his losing many primaries as the primary season concluded.

B. The close race between Obama and Clinton divided Democrats, thus weakening Obama's chances.

C. Obama can't win white working-class and Hispanic voters.

IV. Who will win? I don't know, but . . .

A. If McCain is going to win, he will need to concentrate on setting himself apart from Bush and showing that he is not a typical Republican.

B. If Obama is going to win, he will need to find a way to win over white working-class and Hispanic voters.

Looking at the outline above, you'll see that there are twelve total topics (Roman numerals) and subtopics (uppercase letters). So we need to come up with a twelve-location journey. To give you a better idea of locations to use, for this particular presentation, I will use locations from my current apartment: front door, cupboard, refrigerator, stove, kitchen sink, microwave, television, coffee table, couch, easy chair, mirror, closet. These locations all have distinct appearances. In other words, I did not choose a bunch of walls that all look the same. When choosing locations for your journeys, I advise you to choose distinct-looking locations in an order in which it would make sense for you to encounter them.

Go ahead and decide on twelve locations from your current residence or another familiar place, such as your office, grocery store, pharmacy, athletic club, transit station, or mall. Review the locations mentally until you are able to recite all twelve of them comfortably from memory by simply taking a mental stroll through the locations in order. Once your journey is ready to go, you can use it to commit the presentation to memory.

Let's memorize the election presentation together now. At the first location of your journey, I'd like you to visualize Obama and McCain boxing each other like it's a heavyweight championship match. Remember that the more senses you involve and the crazier and more outlandish you make what you are experiencing in your mind, the more memorable it's going to be. This scenario at the first location of your journey will remind you to say something to the effect of "Who will win—Obama or McCain?" Please note that what you end up saying to your audience does not need to *exactly* match what's in your outline. What you are doing by attaching imagery to the various locations of your journey is creating mental "cue cards" to simply remind you of the point you are trying to get across to your audience. It is fine to use different wording each time you give your presentation, as long as you effectively communicate the point you are trying to make.

At the next location of your journey, visualize McCain riding on a donkey (the Democrats' mascot) with a giant *X* on top of him, as if he's being crossed out. That should be enough to remind you to say something close to "Democrats say that McCain can't win." Again, don't worry if what you end up saying doesn't match your outline exactly.

At your journey's third location, I'd like you to picture Bush shooting a branding iron at the location. This funny scenario should help you to say something similar to "The Republican brand has been shot by Bush, so the Republican candidate can't win this election."

At your journey's next location, visualize George W. Bush doing a celebration dance while holding up three fingers. This will help you to remember the point about a McCain win being, in essence, a third term for Bush.

Your subsequent journey location has McCain walking around with a cane. This should remind you to let your audience know the Democrats say McCain is too old to be president.

At the next location of your journey, picture Obama looking very sad with a bunch of giant elephants (the Republican mascot) surrounding him. This will prompt you to say something like "The Republicans say that Obama can't win."

At the following location, you see Obama with the ground underneath him becoming very loose until he starts to sink while looking up at Hillary Clinton. This will remind you to let your audience know that at the end of the primaries "Obama lost ground to Clinton."

At the next location of your journey, visualize a large group of Democrats suddenly getting split into two groups because a chasm has opened up in the ground, splitting them apart. This will easily remind you of the point you want to make that the Democratic Party is divided.

Moving on to the next location of your journey, you see a bunch of white, working-class voters and Hispanic voters holding up anti-Obama signs. This will remind you to let your audience know that Obama lacks support among these demographics.

Your journey's subsequent location is covered with a bunch of owls yelling out, "Who! Who!" That will be enough to get you to "Who will win? I don't know but . . ."

At your next location, you see McCain and Bush connected to each other like conjoined twins, with McCain struggling to separate himself. This will cue you to explain to your audience, "McCain needs to separate himself from Bush and show that he is not a typical Republican."

At the last location of your journey, the same white working-class and Hispanic voters from earlier are now holding up signs showing that they strongly support Obama. Thinking of this image will allow you to conclude your presentation with something to the effect of "If Obama is to win, he needs to win over white working-class and Hispanic voters."

You should now be able to give the presentation from memory, hitting on every point in order, by simply taking a mental stroll through the locations of your journey and seeing the imagery that you've placed at each location. If you're having difficulty remembering any of the points, simply adjust the imagery at the corresponding location of your journey. Of course, the more you review your journey and the images at their various locations, the more smoothly you'll be able to give your presentation from memory without notes.

You've just started to develop an incredibly valuable skill. Speaking in public is a common fear for many people. No longer will this be so for you!

You may be an office manager or an executive who needs to give a presentation in front of your staff or the board of directors,

TIP When you're committing a speech or presentation to memory, it's important not to get caught up in trying to memorize the entire thing word for word. If you were to recite your speech perfectly from memory, it would come off as monotonous and sound to your audience as though you were reading from a script. You only need mental cues to remind yourself of the points on your outline, and then to effectively communicate the points to your audience.

a Little League manager who must speak to a roomful of parents, an amateur inventor who needs to present an idea to a meeting of venture capitalists, or a consultant giving a presentation to prospective clients. Or maybe you're on a tour for a book you recently published and now have to give a talk before signing autographs.

Just continue to practice what you've learned in this short chapter and you'll soon be impressing and persuading like Cicero!

3

LIFE'S A JOURNEY

In the previous chapter, I introduced you to the journey method with one of its most famous applications—giving speeches like Cicero. We're now going to continue to have fun with this powerful technique, so that you see how it can help you in just about any area of your life. Once you've put in a bit of practice creating journeys and using them as mental filing cabinets to store information, you'll soon realize that you are able to memorize even large bodies of data with ease.

MORE PRESIDENTIAL MEMORIES

In chapter 2, you came up with a journey consisting of twelve different locations from a place you're familiar with, such as your house or apartment. Now I'd like you to imagine only ten different locations from a different place with which you're familiar. If you used your house or apartment for the presentation in chapter 2, this time use another place, such as your office. Go ahead and write down the ten locations. Label the collection of locations OFFICE JOURNEY if you used your office, GROCERY JOURNEY if you used your grocery store, and so forth. I recommend that at some point you keep a journal where you record all your journeys, but it's not necessary to do that at this point. For now, just be sure you can mentally traverse all ten locations of this latest journey—in order, from memory—before you continue.

Now that you have your latest ten-location journey ready to go, we are going to use it to memorize the first ten presidents of the United States. This will be a fun and useful exercise to give you more practice with the journey method. At the first location of your journey, I'd like you to picture a gigantic washing machine that is overflowing. This washing machine should be enough to remind you of **George Washington**. (This first location is more of a formality—there's a very good chance you already know the name of the first U.S. president!)

You now see the characters from *The Addams Family* doing jumping jacks at the second location of your journey. This will remind you of **John Adams**.

At the next location of your journey, you see Geoffrey (the Toys"Я"Us® giraffe) playing with his son. Geoffrey and his son will remind you of **Thomas Jefferson**.

The fourth location of your journey is completely covered with medicine! This medicine is going to remind you of **James Madison**.

Dancing around at the next location of your journey is Marilyn Monroe. Seeing her there will surely remind you of **James Monroe**.

The members of *The Addams Family* are squinting as they try to read something at the next location of your journey. Yes, this will once again remind you of **Adams**. (And the squinty Addams family will help you remember that this is **John Quincy Adams**, instead of John Adams.)

At your journey's next location, you see Michael Jackson doing the moonwalk! There he is, in his famous white glove, strutting along while not going anywhere. This should easily remind you of **Andrew Jackson**.

A van suddenly crashes into the following location of your

journey and a bureau falls out of it. The van with a bureau will remind you of **Martin Van Buren**.

Your journey's next location is getting covered in hair that's being shed by your friend's son, whom you imagine as very hairy. This hairy son will remind you of **William Henry Harrison**.

At the subsequent location of your journey, you see a gigantic old-style rotary phone with a round dialer. This dialer suddenly flies off the phone. The dialer will remind you of **John Tyler**.

Simply read through the paragraphs above one more time and try your best to visualize and vividly experience everything happening at the various locations of your journey. Remember to approach this more as a fun exercise in using your creativity and imagination than as a memory exercise. Smiling and laughing to yourself while going through the exercise is a good sign that you're doing things properly. The more outrageous or hilarious your image, the easier it will be to generate it and remember it.

You should now be able to name the first ten presidents of the United States in order simply by taking a mental stroll through your journey.

TIP As you practice the journey method, along with all the other techniques in this book, you'll begin to notice an improvement in your ability to quickly and easily create vivid images and scenarios in your mind. In addition, you'll be able to see the images in your mind more clearly. The images will become more lifelike. At that point, you'll know that real physical changes have occurred in your brain. You will have built up "mental muscle."

CINEMATIC MEMORIES

I hope that you're starting to realize just how powerful and useful the journey method can be. Let's now continue our exploration of the journey method with another fun exercise. You'll need a fresh new twenty-location journey this time, so that we can memorize the following list of Academy Award winners for Best Picture:

1997—*Titanic*

1998—*Shakespeare in Love*

1999—*American Beauty*

2000—*Gladiator*

2001—*A Beautiful Mind*

2002—*Chicago*

2003—*The Lord of the Rings: The Return of the King*

2004—*Million Dollar Baby*

2005—*Crash*

2006—*The Departed*

2007—*No Country for Old Men*

2008—*Slumdog Millionaire*

2009—*The Hurt Locker*

2010—*The King's Speech*

2011—*The Artist*

2012—*Argo*

2013—*12 Years a Slave*

2014—*Birdman or (The Unexpected Virtue of Ignorance)*

2015—*Spotlight*

2016—*Moonlight*

At the first location of your new twenty-location journey, you see something really unusual! It's a tiny model of the *Titanic*, but there appear to be real people inside it. The *Titanic* is moving around the location, but it runs into an iceberg! You can see all the tiny people jumping out of the ship and hear them screaming. Of course, this scenario recalls *Titanic*.

A man is standing at your next location. You think to yourself, how in the world did he get in here? He's dressed in Shakespearean-era clothing and is reading poetry, about which he seems to be very emotional. Why is he doing this? Because he's in love! Think of this scenario as being *Shakespeare in Love*.

At the following location along your journey, you see a beautiful woman. She appears to be dressed as a beauty contest contestant. You see her posing for the judges. Across her chest is a sash that reads "American Beauty." This scenario calls to mind *American Beauty*.

Standing at your next location is a gladiator. He is trying to pry out a shield, sword, and mace, each of which you see lodged into different parts of the location. You ask him what he is doing and he tells you that he is preparing for battle, because he is a gladiator. Of course, the movie this recalls is *Gladiator*.

You are sort of disgusted at first by what you see at your subsequent location. It's a giant brain. For some strange reason, though, you feel compelled to examine it further. There is something beautiful about its shape and form. You start to envision it as being a very beautiful mind, and even start to stroke it. It feels smooth and strange. That scenario evokes *A Beautiful Mind*.

You are tremendously excited by what you see at your next location—a Chicago-style pizza! You take a slice and start to scarf it down. Delicious! Think of this as *Chicago*.

At the following location, you see a strange, glowing ring. All of a sudden, a man puts on the ring. The man starts to glow as well! The ring on his hand suddenly splits into many rings. The man starts to speak to you in an eerie voice and tells you he is *The Lord of the Rings*.

There is a baby crawling around at your next location. This baby is wearing a diaper filled with cash! My goodness, you think to yourself, that must be about a million dollars stuffed into that baby's diaper. As the baby crawls around, you see the cash start to spew from her diaper. Think of that baby as the *Million Dollar Baby*.

At your subsequent location, there are a bunch of model cars. The cars are facing one another and revving their engines. All of a sudden, they drive at one another at full speed and there is a huge crash. It's the loudest, most explosive crash you've ever witnessed. That scenario calls to mind *Crash*.

Your next location is lined with coffins. How strange and eerie! Even though you are scared, you decide to open one of the coffins. Sure enough, inside you find one of the departed. Think of that whole experience as being *The Departed*.

A group of old men are gathered around a record player, listening to country music, at the following location on your journey. Suddenly an angry man comes around the corner and smashes the record. He shouts, "No country for old men!" That scenario recalls *No Country for Old Men*.

Next, imagine that a dog in tattered clothing appears before you. It looks like it's from a slum, but the dog fetches piles of jewelry and other expensive items for you, because this particular slumdog is actually a millionaire. It's *Slumdog Millionaire*.

There's a giant locker at the next location. You are curious as to what's inside, so you try to force it open, even though it's locked. You keep trying to force it open until you finally hurt yourself. Maybe you break a fingernail. Or sprain a thumb. In any case, you get hurt by the locker, which will make you remember *The Hurt Locker*.

A king runs in place at the next location. You can see his crown shining and are bewildered to see him giving a speech into a microphone while he's running. It's *The King's Speech*.

In the following location, you see an artist painting beautiful artwork right onto the location. The artist is quickly bringing the painting to life. The artwork is so beautiful that you won't soon forget *The Artist*.

Now you see a bunch of giant boxes at the next location. At first they look like cargo boxes, but written on each one is a giant *R*—because they aren't cargo; they're "R-go." Guess what movie? Yes, it's *Argo*!

You see a slave at the next location dressed in tatters. The slave has a carton of eggs and counts one egg for each year he's been a slave: twelve eggs for twelve years. This will remind you of *12 Years a Slave*.

You now see a strange-looking man at your journey's subsequent location. He has giant, birdlike wings attached to his back, and he suddenly starts to fly. He is *Birdman*!

At the next location of your journey, you see a giant light, like the kind they use at movie premieres, brightly illuminating the entire location. Suddenly it turns and shines on you, hurting your eyes. This will easily remind you of *Spotlight*.

Finally, at the last location of your journey, everything is at first very dark and difficult to see. Slowly, the location starts to become more and more illuminated and you notice that this is caused by light from a full moon. This imagery will help you recall *Moonlight*.

You should now be able to recall the last twenty Best Picture winners merely by thinking of each location on your journey. Knowing that we started in 1997, you can easily call to mind that *Titanic* won the Academy Award for Best Picture that year.

Who won in 1999? In order to answer that question, just mentally go to the third location on your journey. The beauty contestant should come to mind, reminding you that *American Beauty* won the Academy Award for Best Picture in 1999.

The exercises in this chapter pull together many of the techniques you've learned so far in this book. The tools you've acquired can be applied to learning more than just random words, but *any* type of information you want to remember. You merely need to create an image or a series of images that represent the information you want to remember, and then link those images to familiar locations.

As you practice, along with improving your visualization techniques, you will develop a stronger and more powerful imagination. Your skills will have reached the point where you will be able to create your own *purely imaginary* journeys. That is to say, you will be able to create journeys that exist solely in your mind, and not in the real world. Matteo Ricci, an Italian missionary, introduced this technique to China in 1596 in his book *Treatise on Mnemonic Arts* (written in Chinese). He called these purely imaginary journeys "memory palaces."

For instance, you might imagine a castle. At the front of the castle is a drawbridge. After passing over the drawbridge, you reach a giant castle door. When you open the door, there is a long red carpet. The red carpet leads to a staircase, and so forth. As you mentally review the castle that you've created in your imagination, it will eventually become a real place in your mind. You will be able to use that imaginary castle and the locations within it to store images and information, just as you learned to do with a journey through a real-world location, such as your residence.

You now have a solid handle on the journey method and how it can be applied in multiple ways and situations. Of course, as with anything else in life, the more you practice, the better you will get at it, and the more improvement you will see. As you can no doubt tell from going through these exercises, this practice is also wonderful exercise for your brain.

REMEMBER NAMES
LIKE A POLITICIAN

4

It's no secret that remembering people's names and other things about them can help you become a more likable and popular person. It shows people that you care about and are interested in them. Politicians, in particular, recognize the power this ability confers. In fact, I've been hired by politicians on numerous occasions to help them hone this important skill.

When politicians attend fund-raisers, they want to know as much as possible about the attendees: their names, their spouses' names, causes they support, causes they don't support, and more. Politicians also realize that if you fail to remember people's names or, perhaps even worse, call them by the wrong name, this can be detrimental to developing positive relationships. Mistakes like this can have a negative impact on your likability and popularity over time. Although I use the example of politicians to illustrate the importance of becoming better at remembering names, hopefully you realize that this skill can be an asset to you in just about any career as well as in your personal life.

WHAT'S IN A NAME?

"I'm horrible at remembering names, but I never forget a face."
You've probably heard a thought like that uttered by many people
over the years. That's because it's common for people to be good
at remembering faces but not names. At some point in your life,
you've probably seen someone whom you may have met many
years in the past. You immediately recognized the person's face,
but no matter how hard you tried, you weren't able to recall his
name. Or, let's say you attend a party with a friend of yours, where
you both meet a lot of new people. Two weeks after the party, your
friend asks, "Do you remember that attorney we met at the party
who is also a member of the tennis club?" Given just that brief
description, you and your friend can both picture what that person
looked like; however, neither one of you can manage to recall the
person's name. This is also common.

We experience situations like these because when we meet
people we *see* their face, but at no point do we *see* their name.
A name is something much more abstract, to which we cannot
easily relate. Remember: In previous chapters you learned that
we remember things that we can see and picture. I open my
presentations around the world by naming hundreds of people in
the audience after having heard each person's name only once. I
accomplish this in part by turning each person's name into vivid
imagery I can easily see and picture in my mind. You're about to
learn to do the same thing, and become better than you ever were
before at remembering people's names.

PAY ATTENTION

Before I start to help you turn names into vivid imagery, I'd like
to address one other common issue that affects our ability to
remember names: focus and attention. I realize this may seem
obvious, but oftentimes, when we are introduced to someone, we

> **TIP** Believe it or not, just like humans, crows have an amazing ability to remember people's faces and link them to memories and experiences. So don't pester a crow: Months later that same bird might try to dive-bomb you!

are paying no attention to her name whatsoever. Our mind is on anything and everything at that moment other than the person's name. But to remember someone's name, you simply must *focus* on it for at least one to two seconds.

The following procedure will help you to do this:

1. **Immediately repeat the name and shake the person's hand.** If you are introduced to someone named Tim, say something to the effect of, "Nice to meet you, Tim," or "Pleased to meet you, Tim." You might even say the name first: "Tim, so nice to meet you." If possible, shake Tim's hand while saying this. This forces you to focus and pay attention to the name.

2. **Early in your interaction, use the person's name in any simple question.** "So, Tim, how do you know Chester?" or "Tim, what brings you to the meeting today?" are examples of this technique. I want to emphasize here that I am only recommending that you ask *one* simple question using the person's name early on in your interaction. It is not necessary, and I do *not* recommend, that you use the person's name repeatedly during your conversation. One simple question using the name will suffice to help keep it in your mind and prevent it from going in one ear and out the other.

3. **Think of a connection between the person's name and anything you already know.** I really do mean *anything*. The name Tim might make you think of Tiny Tim, Senator Tim Kaine, the actor Tim Allen, or it could even simply be that you have a friend or a family member who is also named Tim. Connecting the name to something or someone you already know will help the name to stick in your mind.

4. **Say goodbye using the person's name.** Before you leave the party, meeting, wedding, or whatever type of function you may be attending, make sure to say goodbye to the people you've met, using their names. A simple "Goodbye, John" or "Until next time, John" or "Nice talking with you, John" will go a long way toward cementing the name in your mind and give you a much better chance of remembering it the next time you see the person.

The procedure I've outlined above should be fairly easy for you to put into practice right away. It will help you focus on people's names when you meet them and take control of social interactions when being introduced to people. If someone introduces you to a group of people in rapid succession—Jim, Dorothy, Damien, Liza, Tim, and so on—remembering the names may become difficult, even for someone at my skill level. I recommend that you try to take control and slow down the process by at least implementing the first step above. If this isn't possible, you could even implement the steps immediately following the rapid-fire introductions. In this situation, it's perfectly acceptable to ask for a person's name again or verify it while starting with the first step: "You were Tim, correct?" or "I'm sorry, I missed your name given the rapid introductions, you were . . . ?" Then, continue with the remaining steps as best as you can.

IMAGINE THAT

In chapter 1, you learned to link images to locations on your body. You can follow a similar technique to help you remember a person's name; however, in this case the images will go on the other person's body instead of your own. When you meet someone, ask yourself how this particular person looks unique to you. This unique characteristic could be a particular facial feature or something about his overall appearance. Once you've decided on the unique aspect, you'll want to exaggerate it in your mind in some way. This exaggerated feature will now serve as the storage place for the person's name.

Next, think of an image that will in some way, *any* way, remind you of the name. The association might be based on sound. For instance, the Sahara might remind you of the name *Sarah*. A wave might remind you of *Dave*. Alternatively, your images might be more symbolic. A white rabbit could remind you of *Alice*. There might even be an intermediate connection in your mind, such as using a dumbbell that you would encounter in a gym to remind you of the name *Jim*. (Don't worry. I've never said, "Pleased to meet you, dumbbell," and I'm sure you won't, either. Your brain knows better.)

There are various ways an image might remind you of a particular name. Once you've decided on your image, simply use your imagination to vividly link the image to the unique aspect of the person. While linking the image to the person, try to incorporate what you've learned earlier in this book: See the imagery as vividly as you can, involving additional senses, and try to make all of this as crazy, unusual, and extraordinary as possible.

Let's jump into an example using imagery, along with a unique aspect of a person's appearance, to memorize the person's name. If you meet a guy named John who, in your opinion, has large ears, you might imagine his ears as gigantic and see them swinging from the sides of his head. Next, you might visualize a toilet bowl (John) twirling around in each of his ears! A toilet bowl would remind you of going to the *John*. Unflattering images might in some cases be the most memorable to you, so go ahead and use them. People will not know how you remember their name. They'll only notice that you've taken the time to learn it and will very much appreciate that fact. If you vividly experience the imagery with the ears and the toilet bowl in your mind, the next time you see John, you'll once again notice his ears, as you did before, and all the vivid imagery will immediately come back to your mind, prompting you to remember his name.

What if you meet a woman named Jane with a distinctive hairstyle? You might visualize a thick metal chain appearing and braiding itself into her hair. *Chain* will easily remind you of *Jane*. It might help make the scene easier to remember if you imagine the chain causing the hair to emit a pleasant shampoo smell. Take a few seconds to vividly experience this happening, and I'm certain that the next time you see Jane you will immediately remember her name. Note that the image could be a person with the same name, instead of an object. So instead of seeing a chain, you might imagine Jane Fonda becoming entwined in Jane's hair.

The key is to unleash your imagination and experience all of this as if it were actually happening. It will take practice, but soon you'll be doing this easily and having a great time.

SAME NAME GAME

An alternative way to commit a person's name to memory is to take the unique feature you've exaggerated in your mind and mentally place that aspect on someone you already know with the same name. Let me illustrate how this would work with John and Jane, discussed above.

Instead of putting a toilet bowl in each of John's giant ears swinging from the side of his head, simply visualize a friend of yours named John having these giant ears swinging from the side of *his* head. If you vividly experience the sight of your *friend John* with those giant swinging ears, then the next time you see *new John*, upon noticing his ears once again you'll immediately remember that you placed those ears on your *friend John*—thus this new person's name is John as well. With Jane, we imagined that her hair was growing longer and thicker, and giving off a pleasant smell. Simply imagine this same thing happening to a *friend of yours named Jane*. When you later see the *new Jane* you just met, you should once again notice her hair, as you did before. The imagery of the hair growing out with the pleasant smell will return to your mind. Then, just ask yourself where you placed that unique hair. You'll immediately remember that you visualized it on your *friend Jane*; thus this new woman's name is also Jane!

Another option for effectively committing a person's name to memory is to focus on how this person in some way looks like someone you already know with the same name. The person you already know doesn't necessarily need to be someone you know *personally*. It could be a famous person or even a character from a popular TV show or movie. Upon meeting a person named Donald and asking yourself how he looks unique to you, you might notice that he has a nose that looks a lot like Donald Sutherland's nose. Focusing on that physical similarity between the two Donalds might be enough to lock this new Donald's name into your mind. However, I'd recommend taking it one step further. After focusing on the similar-looking noses, I'd visualize Donald Sutherland morphing into a new version of himself—turning into this new guy you've just met named Donald. If you vividly experience this happening in your mind, upon once again seeing the Donald you've recently met, you'll immediately notice his nose, as you did before. This will trigger the memory of Donald Sutherland morphing into him, and you'll know that this new person's name is also Donald.

With the example of Donald, we focused on a particular facial feature, but keep in mind that you can instead focus on an aspect of the person's overall appearance. If you meet someone named Arnold who is extremely muscular, like Arnold Schwarzenegger, you might imagine Arnold Schwarzenegger morphing into this new person who is also named Arnold.

PUTTING IT TOGETHER

Let's review the techniques for remembering names that I've covered:

1. Focus on something unique about the person, exaggerate it, and then place an image in your mind that will remind you of the person's name.

2. Focus on something unique about the person, exaggerate it, and then mentally place that exaggerated aspect on someone you already know with the same name.

3. Focus on a physical similarity between the person you're meeting and someone you already know while visualizing one person morphing into the other.

These techniques for remembering names will take some practice, but after using them for three or four weeks you will dramatically improve your ability to remember the names of people you meet.

> **TIP** When first starting out with these visual-based techniques, you may find that it takes you longer than you'd like to come up with images to remind you of certain names. This is perfectly normal; it happened to me when I started out as well. Trust that, with practice, you'll increase the speed at which you create images.

If you stick to your memory training, over time images for certain names may automatically pop into your head. This can be very useful. Below, I've provided you with images that you might want to use regularly for some common names. It would be a great exercise to edit and add to the list as you please.

MEN'S NAMES

BILL = dollar bill, bull, Bill Clinton

BRIAN = brain, bran, Bryan Cranston

CHARLES = charred Ls, twirls, Prince Charles

CHRISTOPHER = Christ with fur, Christopher Reeve, Christopher Columbus

DANIEL = doe in the Nile, Daniel Craig, Daniel Radcliffe

DAVID = statue of David, David Beckham, David Bowie

DONALD = dough nailed, Donald Trump, Donald Duck

ED = education, Ed McMahon, Ed Sheeran

GEORGE = gorge, Curious George, George Bush

JAMES = jam(s), James Franco, shelf of games

JEFF = giraffe, Jif® peanut butter, Jeff Bridges

JOHN = toilet bowl, John F. Kennedy, John Travolta

JOSEPH = joe (coffee) siphon, Joseph Stalin, Joseph Gordon-Levitt

KEN = Ken doll, can, Ken Norton

MARK = marker, scuff mark, Mark Twain

MATT = welcome mat, Matt Dillon, Matt Damon

MICHAEL = mic with an L-shaped handle, Michael Jackson, the archangel Michael

PAUL = pill, pole, Paul McCartney

RICHARD = rich orchard, rice chard, Richard Branson

RICK = a wreck, rook, Rick Moranis

ROBERT = robber, Robert Redford, Robert De Niro

RON = run, rune, Ron Howard

STEVEN = stew in a van, stove with N coming out, Steven Spielberg

THOMAS = English muffin, toe mess, Thomas Edison

WILLIAM = wheel made of ham, William Shakespeare, Prince William

WOMEN'S NAMES

BARBARA = barber, barbed wire, Barbra Streisand

BETTY = casino chips (bet), bat tea, Betty Boop

CAROL = a Christmas carol, car rolling (car-roll), Carol Burnett

DONNA = doughnut, the dawn nodding (dawn-nod), Donna Karan

DOROTHY = yellow brick road, Dorothy with Toto, Dorothy Dandridge

ELIZABETH = Z on bet (Z-bet), lice making a bet (lice-bet), Elizabeth Taylor

HELEN = a thousand ships (Helen of Troy), healing, Helen Mirren

JANE = chain, Jane from *Tarzan*, Jane Fonda

JANET = a J-shaped net (J-net), a net made of chains (chain-net), Janet Jackson

JENNIFER = gin with fur on it (gin-fur), Jennifer Garner, Jennifer Aniston

KAREN = carrying something, corn, Karen Gillan

LINDA = *linda* in Spanish (beautiful), Linda Ronstadt, Lynda Carter

LISA = lease with an A, Lisa Simpson, *Mona Lisa*

MARGARET = margarita, Margaret Cho, Margaret Thatcher

MARIA = marrying an A, scene from *West Side Story*, Maria Sharapova

MARY = wedding, *Mary Poppins*, Virgin Mary

MELANIE = a melon, melon on a knee (melon-knee), Melanie Griffith

MONICA = a harmonica, moniker, Monica Lewinsky

NANCY = naan in the sea, Nancy Reagan, Nancy Pelosi

PATRICIA = pat on the back, pat of butter on rice (pat-rice), Patricia Arquette

RUTH = root, Baby Ruth, Dr. Ruth

SANDRA = sand straw, Santa drawing (Santa-draw), Sandra Bullock

SHARON = Cher in something, sharing, Sharon Stone

STEPHANIE = stuffing honey (stuff-honey), step on a penny (step-penny), Stephanie Seymour

SUSAN = sue someone, sew sand, Susan Sarandon

Practicing what you've learned in this chapter will give you more power in your personal and professional life because you'll be able to build better relationships with clients, colleagues, and anyone else you meet. You may not have any interest in entering politics, but your ability to better remember names will soon make you a more likable and popular person.

Enjoy it and have fun!

5

NUMBERS ARE ALL AROUND US

We are all frequently faced with the need to remember numerical information: phone numbers, dates, addresses, passwords, prices, formulas, facts that contain figures, and more. Numbers are indeed all around us! All the techniques you learned in chapter 1 can help you remember numbers; however, there is an intermediate step you must take. Before you can apply what you've learned to the task of remembering numbers, you must first learn to turn any number or sequence of numbers into an image.

THE PHONETIC ALPHABET SYSTEM

You are about to learn the most powerful system ever created for turning numbers into images. Many different versions of this system have been developed over the centuries, but the particular version that I'll cover here was created about three hundred years ago and is often attributed to Stanislaus Mink von Wennsshein, the pseudonym of Johann Just Winckelmann (1620–1699), a German writer and historian. In my experience, it is the easiest version to learn. Over the course of history, this system has been called the major system, the phonetic mnemonic, and the phonetic alphabet system. In this book, I will refer to it as the *phonetic alphabet system*, because I feel that name most accurately describes how the system works.

The phonetic alphabet system applies one or more consonant sounds to the numbers 0 through 9. You can then use vowel sounds anywhere to help you form words from number sequences. I realize this may seem a bit confusing at first, but bear with me; the system will become clearer with examples. For most people, this chapter will probably be the most difficult to grasp and require the most work upfront to fully master, but the investment in time to learn this system will be well worth it. It will make memorizing any type of information that contains numbers a breeze! Let's take a look at the chart below that outlines the incredibly useful phonetic alphabet system.

Numbers	Sounds	Hints/Associations
0	s, z	Zero
1	t, d	1 Downstroke (ta-da)
2	n	2 Downstrokes
3	m	3 Downstrokes
4	r	four
5	L	High Five
6	ch, sh, j	6 & J both have hook shape
7	k, g	K
8	f, v	eight in middle
9	p, b	9 looks like an upside down b or p

The first two columns of the chart list the numbers 0–9 and the corresponding phonetic sounds for each number. For the number 0, the sounds are *s* and *z*. These are the phonetic sounds made by *s* as in *sock* and *z* as in *zoo*. Keep this idea of phonetic sounds in mind as I go through the rest of the numbers and corresponding sounds. When memorizing the consonant sounds, many find it helpful to pronounce them as syllables (like *sah* and *zah*) for ease of saying them aloud.

For the number 1, the sounds are *t* and *d*. For the number 2, the sound is *n*. For the number 3, the sound is *m*. For the number 4, the sound is *r*. For the number 5, the sound is *l* (ell). For the number 6, the sounds are *ch*, *sh*, and *j*. For the number 7, the sounds are *k* and *g*. The *g*-sound here for the number 7 is the hard *g*-sound as in the words *gas* or *Gus*. The soft *g*-sound, as in the words *gel* or *giraffe*, would correspond to the number 6 because that number has the *j* sound in this system. For the number 8, the sounds are *f* and *v*. For the number 9, the sounds are *p* and *b*.

I want to emphasize that this system is all about the sounds or *phonetics*, thus the name *phonetic* alphabet system. This system doesn't have much to do with the letters. I've only provided letters in the chart to help you learn the phonetic sounds for each number. Knowing the sounds for each number is the end goal when studying this system. Before I go over the third column in the chart, which has been designed to help you commit the numbers and corresponding sounds to memory, I'll go over some exercises to make sure you understand what we've covered so far.

Given the number 37, what are some possible corresponding words? At this point, feel free to refer to the chart for help. Remember that you can use vowel sounds anywhere to help you form words. You just need to be sure that your word begins with the *m*-sound and ends with either the *k*- or *g*-sound.

Some possible words for 37 could be: *mic*, *Mike*, *mug*, or *Mick*. You may have come up with many more possibilities. Although it's not essential, I highly recommend using nouns whenever possible.

This is because it's much easier to picture a person, place, or thing, as opposed to something more abstract. Also, when you later see the image in your mind, there will be no mistaking what you are seeing. For instance, if you pictured the word *make* for 37, later you might get confused, wondering if you are looking at an image for *make*, *create*, or *build*, since images you might visualize to remind you of those words could all be very similar. However, if you picture someone you know named *Mike*, you'll know exactly who you are seeing in your mind.

Given the number 40, what are some possible corresponding words?

You might have come up with *rose*, *Ross*, or *Russ*. I'd like to point out that the word *rice* would perfectly correspond to the number 40 as well. Although you won't find a *c* anywhere in the chart, remember that this is all about phonetics. The consonant sounds in the word *rice* are *r* and *s*, which correspond to 40.

Given the word *door*, what is the corresponding number? Looking at the chart should help you to realize that *door* corresponds to 14, because the consonant sounds in *door* are *d* and *r*.

What number does the word *bike* correspond to? The consonant sounds in *bike* are *b* and *k*, so the number should be 97.

What about the word *glass*? Hopefully, you realize that *glass* corresponds to 750. The consonant sounds in *glass* are *g*, *l*, and *s*. *Glass* does not correspond to *7,500*, even though there are two *s*'s in the word *glass*. This is because we only pronounce the *s*-sound in *glass* one time and, again, this system is about *phonetics*, not spelling.

MEMORY HELPERS

At this point, you should have a good understanding of how the phonetic alphabet system works. The next step is for you to memorize the chart. I've provided some hints and associations in the chart's third column to help you with this. Let's go over them now.

In the first row, you'll see *Zero*. It should be clear that this word begins with the *z*-sound (*z*), and ends with an *o*, which should remind you of a 0. Keeping this in mind should help you remember that for the number 0, the corresponding sound is *z*. If you can remember the *z*-sound for 0, then it should be fairly easy to remember the *s*-sound as well, because that is the only sound in the chart that is similar to the *z*-sound. When you vocalize both the *z*- and *s*-sounds, your mouth and tongue position remain the same. Try it now: Vocalize the *z*-sound out loud while noting your mouth and tongue position. Now, do the same thing for the *s*-sound. You'll note that the mouth and tongue positions do not change. This is the case for all sounds that are on the same row in the chart. So, your mouth and tongue position will remain the same when producing the *t*-sound as when you produce the *d*-sound.

The second row of the chart shows *1 downstroke* in the third column. On a sheet of scrap paper, write the letter *t* and note how many times your pen makes a downstroke. It should be only one time. Do the same now for a *d* and you'll note that there is also only one downstroke. Keeping this in mind should help you to remember that, for the number 1, the sounds are *t* and *d*. It may also be useful to think of the exclamation "Ta-da!" to help you remember that the *t* and *d* sounds go together in the chart.

The third row of the chart shows *2 downstrokes* in the third column. On a sheet of scrap paper, write the letter *n* and note how many times your pen makes a downstroke. It should be two times. Keeping this in mind should help you remember that, for the number 2, the corresponding sound is *n*.

The fourth row of the chart shows *3 downstrokes* in the third column. On a sheet of scrap paper, write the letter *m* and note how many times your pen makes a downstroke. It should be three times. Keeping this in mind should help you remember that, for the number 3, the corresponding sound is *m*.

The fifth row of the chart shows the word *four* in the third column with emphasis on the *r* at the end of the word. It's clear that the word *four* ends with the *r*-sound. This will help you to remember that the number 4 corresponds to *r*.

The sixth row of the chart shows a hand giving a *high five* in the third column. You can see that the index finger and thumb of the hand form what looks like an *L* shape. Thinking of this will serve to remind you that for the number 5 the corresponding sound is *l* (ell).

In the third column of the next row in the chart, you'll see that I've indicated that the number 6 and the letter *J* both have a hook shape to them when written. On a sheet of scrap paper, write down a number 6 with an exaggerated hook shape. Next to that, write out a capital *J* with an exaggerated hook shape. This should help cement in your mind the connection between a 6 and the letter *J*, and thus fix in your mind that *j* corresponds to the number 6. I recommend that you start by learning the *j*-sound for 6 and then later move on to the *ch* and *sh* sounds, which are similar and produced with the same mouth and tongue positions.

In the third column of the following row in the chart, you'll see that I've depicted a *K* drawn so that you can see a 7 on the left side of the *K* and another 7 on the right side of the *K* that is oriented differently. Two 7s with the correct orientation can be joined together to form the letter *K*. This should help you to remember that, for the number 7, the corresponding sound is *k*. I recommend that you start by learning the *k*-sound for 7 and then later move on to the *g*-sound, which is similar and produced with the same mouth and tongue position. It may also be useful to think of the word *keg*, since it contains both the *k*- and *g*-sounds.

In the third column of the next row in the chart, you'll find a lowercase scripted or cursive letter *f*. You should be able to see what sort of looks like an 8 in the middle of this *f* constructed by the two loops. Thinking about the two loops in the middle of the *f* that together look like an 8 will help you remember that for the number 8, the corresponding sound is *f*. I recommend that you start with learning the *f*-sound for 8 and then later move on to the v-sound, which is similar and produced with the same mouth and tongue position. It may also be helpful to think of the vegetable juice product called V8®.

In the third column of the last row in the chart, you'll see that I've indicated that different orientations of the number 9 can form the letters p and b. On a sheet of scrap paper, write down the number 9. Now, simply imagine flipping that 9 over horizontally and you'll see a p. Next, flip that p up and you'll see a b. Thinking about doing this with the number 9 will help you remember that, for the number 9, the corresponding sounds are p and b. It might be useful to think of peanut butter in order to remember that the p and b sounds go together in the chart.

I recommend that you take at least fifteen minutes to review the phonetic alphabet system chart before continuing to read this chapter. Make sure to use the hints and associations from the third column, along with my explanations above, to guide you. Once you feel comfortable reciting each digit, along with its corresponding sounds, from memory, you can then continue on to the exercises below.

TRY IT YOURSELF

Now that you've had some time to review the chart, I'd like you to attempt the following exercises without referring to it. Use only your memory and creativity.

Please list at least one possible word for the following random numbers:

57 = _____

17 = _____

25 = _____

94 = _____

35 = _____

49 = _____

65 = _____

70 = _____

99 = _____

86 = _____

Here are some potential answers for the above numbers (note these are just a few ideas, with many more possible):

57: lake, lock, leg, or log

17: dog, tack, tick, or duck

25: nail, Nile, null, or Nell

94: bear, pear, bar, or par

35: mail, mall, Mel, or mole

49: wrap, rope, rib, or Rob

65: jail, gel, shell, or Jill

70: case, gas, kiss, or Gus

99: pub, pub, pop, or Bob

86: fish, fudge, voyage, or Fiji

Yes, *voyage* and *Fiji* would be possible words for the number 86. The consonant sounds in the word *Fiji* are f (8) and j (6). Vowel sounds, which do not translate into numbers, can be used anywhere to help you form words, even at the beginning of a word or at its end (such as the vowel sound at the end of *Fiji*). The same goes for the multiple vowel sounds in the middle of *voyage*; for our purposes, a y-sound is always considered a vowel sound.

Next, you're going to determine the numbers that correspond to some random words. In the previous exercise, you could give many possible words for each number. However, in the next exercise, only one possible number can correspond to each word. That is part of the power of the phonetic alphabet system. Images you choose can only correspond to one number sequence, so there will be no confusion as to what number you were trying to remember.

Provide the number that corresponds to each of the random words below:

door = _____

light = _____

book = _____

case = _____

pen = _____

kite = _____

tail = _____

map = _____

sauce = _____

wrench = _____

The answers to the exercise above should be as follows:

door = 14	kite = 71
light = 51	tail = 15
book = 97	map = 39
case = 70	sauce = 00
pen = 92	wrench = 426

MEMORIZING LONG NUMBERS

You're next going to memorize the following long number sequence:

426126645926145941703

Don't worry. I'm going to guide you through the steps, and it will only take you a few minutes to have it perfectly memorized. Just relax, visualize what I describe to you, and, most importantly, have fun!

Imagine that you see a gigantic **wrench** (426) spinning in the air. Attached to one end of this wrench is a delicious **Danish** (126), which is also spinning. **Sheryl** (645) Crow comes along and starts to eat the Danish. She walks backward while eating it and falls onto a **bench** (926). Next, she flies off the bench and is caught by an ugly **troll** (145). A giant **bird** (941) then swallows the troll. The bird then finishes off its meal by drinking a **cosmo** (703). Reread this story one more time while vividly experiencing it in your mind as best you can.

Can you remember the key words (all nouns) from the story? Try to recite them from memory.

They should be **wrench, Danish, Sheryl, bench, troll, bird, cosmo**. Make sure you can recite all the key words from memory by relying on the story before you continue. Once you know the key words from the story, it will be easy to recite the entire twenty-one-digit sequence. When you go through the story from memory, you'll first see a wrench, which will give you 426. You'll next encounter a Danish, which will give you 126. Next up is Sheryl, which is 645. You'll next see a bench, or 926. A troll is the following thing you'll see, and that is 145. Next you'll run across the bird, which is 941. Lastly, you'll envision the cosmo, which is 703. Try to recite the entire number sequence on your own by simply playing through the story in your mind, and translating each key word back into its corresponding number.

Amazing, isn't it? You've just memorized a random twenty-one-digit sequence in a matter of minutes! This is only the beginning! Soon, you will be able to quickly and easily remember any type of information that contains numbers.

Let's move on to memorizing phone numbers. Before the advent of the cell phone, many of us were good at remembering phone numbers. It was common for people to know the numbers of relatives, friends, and businesses that they frequented often. Nowadays, however, people have become so accustomed to entering phone numbers into their phones, and then dialing automatically, that they have difficulty committing even just one phone number to memory. Things have gotten so bad that a lot of people out there don't even know their own phone number! (Imagine being in an automobile accident and not being able to have the paramedic call your family, because your smartphone was damaged and all your phone numbers were in it.) This is a very good example of the "use it or lose it" principle as it applies to memory.

TIP I encourage you to commit to memory as many phone numbers as possible. When you need to dial a phone number, first rely on your memory. If you are unable to recall the number, then go ahead and use the auto dial from your phone's address book. Getting into this habit will help you practice the techniques in this book and is a great daily exercise for your memory.

Let's say your doctor's phone number is 555-0184. When committing someone's number to memory, I always begin my imagery with the person whose number I'm memorizing. So, you might imagine that your doctor picks up an "oily lily" (555). The oil from the lily starts to drip all over your doctor's seat (01). This magically causes a huge fire (84) to start, which burns your doctor as the flames rise from the seat. Take ten seconds or less to picture that happening and it will be locked into your memory. The next time you think of your doctor, you'll remember seeing him pick up an oily lily that dripped onto his seat, causing a huge fire. This will instantly tell you that his number is 555 (oily lily)—01 (seat) 84 (fire)! When dealing with most phone numbers, I don't bother with the area code since I know my city's area code and the area codes of many major cities around the world, because I travel a lot to give speeches. However, if you'd like to memorize the area code, then just add one extra image up front. If your doctor is located in San Francisco, which has an area code of 415, then you might first see your doctor play with a giant rattle (415) before he picks up the oily lily. That's all that's involved!

TIP Note that your brain naturally knows the ordering of a story you've seen, experienced, or explicitly created. If you see your doctor pick up an oily lily, your brain will not mistakenly recall the event as an oily lily picking up your doctor. You can rely on your brain to place the sequence of events in the correct order.

FACTS AND FIGURES

Next, I'll teach you how to memorize any facts that contain figures. Please note that the "facts" and corresponding figures below are not necessarily accurate—and some are completely made up. They are listed solely for the purpose of helping you learn how to memorize similar facts with figures.

1. The price of a nice DVD player at the store is $86.25.

2. The stock price of JAVA is now $13.49.

3. The Korean War started in 1950.

4. The address of the San Francisco Tennis Club is 645 Fifth Street.

5. The number of pairs of shoes that Jennifer Lawrence owns is 127.

The key is to relax and have fun while visualizing and experiencing scenarios that will remind you of the facts and figures above. Images reminding you of the *facts* will interact with images corresponding to the related *figures* or *numbers*. Read through each of the scenarios below twice while doing your best to see and experience what I describe.

1. Picture a DVD player that is covered with fish (86), each with a giant nail (25) going through it.

2. Next picture a cup of java that is being consumed by your friend Tom (13). While Tom is drinking the java, a rope (49) ties itself around him and he struggles to break free.

3. You try to eat some Korean BBQ, but it has a bunch of lace (50) tied all around it.

4. Sheryl (645) Crow picks up and swings a large tennis racket that has 5 treats (Fifth Street) on it.

5. Jennifer Lawrence is showing off all her shoes when she suddenly gets run over by a tank (127)!

Now ask yourself the following questions:

1. What is the price of the DVD player?

2. What is the stock price of JAVA?

3. In what year did the Korean War begin?

4. What is the address of the San Francisco Tennis Club?

5. How many pairs of shoes does Jennifer Lawrence own?

Hopefully, this brief introduction to the phonetic alphabet system has shown you just how easy it can be to remember any type of information that contains numbers. Should you encounter number-related information that I didn't specifically cover in this chapter, with just a little creativity you can easily take what you've learned here and apply it to any situation. Look around and you'll see numbers everywhere. Now, you can remember them all with ease.

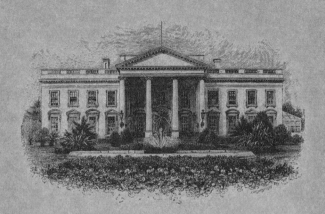

6

FUN WITH THE PRESIDENTS

In the previous chapter, you were introduced to an incredibly powerful system for memorizing any type of information that contains numbers. Amazingly, in addition to making it surprisingly easy to memorize numbers, the phonetic alphabet system can also help you build a virtually limitless amount of mental storage places in which you can file away information for easy retrieval when you need it later on. I'll illustrate how this works later in this chapter by having you complete a fun exercise in which you'll memorize all the United States presidents in order—forward, backward, and by number.

A HUNDRED IMAGES

Before we get to the presidents, let's establish images for all possible number sequences between 0 and 99. You will acquire two important benefits by doing this. First, you'll gain tremendous *speed* in memorizing any type of information that contains numbers. This is because, unlike in the previous chapter, you'll no longer have to come up with images "on the fly" to represent numbers. You will have preset images readily available for you to use. Second, these hundred images (for numbers 00 to 99) can serve as storage places for new information—and associated images—you'd like to learn. I briefly introduced you to this principle with the *peg list* in chapter 1 (page 11).

Following is a list of images that you can visualize to represent the sequences 00 to 99. These are images that I feel work best, based on the phonetic alphabet system and my decades' worth of experience teaching memory techniques. Feel free to change any that you'd like, but be sure to decide on an image for each number and stick with it. That's the only way to gain the level of fluency that will have an image immediately pop into your head upon seeing a number. Use the space to the right of each number-image pairing to make notes you can return to later for review. If you have any difficulty understanding why the images below correspond to their respective numbers, I recommend a quick review of chapter 5 for clarification.

00 = sauce		15 = tail	
01 = suit		16 = Taj (Mahal)	
02 = sun		17 = tack	
03 = (Uncle) Sam		18 = TV (short for television)	
04 = sore		19 = tub	
05 = sail		20 = nose	
06 = sash		21 = net	
07 = sock		22 = nun	
08 = safe		23 = gnome	
09 = soup		24 = Norah (Jones)	
10 = toes		25 = nail	
11 = tot		26 = nacho (cheese)	
12 = tin		27 = Nick (Nolte)	
13 = Tom (Selleck)		28 = knife	
14 = tire		29 = knob	

30 = mouse	65 = shell
31 = Matt (Damon)	66 = Josh
32 = moon	67 = shack
33 = mom	68 = chef
34 = mare	69 = ship
35 = mail	70 = case
36 = match	71 = cat
37 = Mike (Tyson)	72 = cane
38 = movie	73 = comb
39 = mop	74 = car
40 = Rose	75 = coal
41 = Rod	76 = cash
42 = rain	77 = cake
43 = ram	78 = cuff
44 = Rory (McIlroy)	79 = cop
45 = roll	80 = (smiley) face
46 = (Richie) Rich	81 = Fat (Albert)
47 = rook	82 = fan
48 = roof	83 = foam
49 = rope	84 = fire
50 = lace	85 = file
51 = light	86 = fish
52 = lion	87 = fig
53 = lamb	88 = fife
54 = lair	89 = Fabio
55 = lily	90 = bus
56 = leech	91 = bat
57 = lock	92 = bun
58 = leaf	93 = bomb
59 = loop	94 = bear
60 = shoes	95 = bell
61 = sheet	96 = bush
62 = Sean	97 = bike
63 = Shamu	98 = beef
64 = Cher	99 = Bob (Dylan)

Before continuing with this chapter, make sure to review the numbers and corresponding images above. For now, I recommend focusing on the images for numbers 00 to 50. We're about to use your images for 00 to 45 to memorize the U.S. presidents.

IMAGINING THE PRESIDENTS

In the paragraphs that follow, imagine experiencing everything happening as vividly as you can. If you're unfamiliar with anything I describe and have difficulty picturing it, you can do a quick Google search to see a picture, or use your own imagery that will more effectively remind you of that particular president. Let's begin.

You see a nice **suit** (**01**) getting washed in a *washing machine* (Washington). Next, picture the burning hot **sun** (**02**) melting the characters from *The Addams Family* (Adams; that is, John Adams). You now see **Uncle Sam** (**03**) getting into a fight with the rock group *Jefferson Airplane* (Jefferson). Next, you notice a large **sore** (**04**) on your body and have to inject it full of *medicine* (Madison) to make it go away. The wind hitting the **sail** (**05**) of a sailboat is also blowing on the dress of *Marilyn Monroe* (Monroe). A cloth **sash** (**06**) is wrapping itself around the Addams Family (Adams; that is, John Quincy Adams) and they are struggling to break free. *Michael Jackson* (Jackson) is dancing on top of a giant **sock** (**07**). You notice an extremely large **safe** (**08**). A *van* (Van) bursts out of the safe and drops a *bureau* (Buren). *George Harrison* (Harrison) is swimming in a gigantic bowl of **soup** (**09**).

Reread the paragraph above three times while doing your best to clearly visualize and experience everything described as if it were really happening.

Next up, you see some **toes** (**10**) wiggling and dialing an old rotary phone *dialer* (Tyler). You decide to continuously *poke* (Polk) a tater **tot** (**11**) and watch the indentation appear and disappear as you do it. *Elizabeth Taylor* (Taylor) is having fun posing for photos and showing off her new dress that's completely made of **tin** (**12**).

You're amazed to watch **Tom** (**13**) Selleck doing some sort of crazy performance at the *Fillmore* (Fillmore). A sharp metallic object starts to *pierce* (Pierce) a **tire** (**14**) and you watch and feel the air rush out. A long animal **tail** (**15**) wraps itself around *two cannons* (Buchanan) and causes them to fire. Next you find yourself at the **Taj** (**16**) Mahal and are surprised to see *Abraham Lincoln* (Lincoln) giving a speech in front of it. You use a **tack** (**17**) to pry open a bottle of *Johnson's* (Johnson; that is, Andrew Johnson) baby oil and it splatters all over you, causing you to become very slick. On a large-screen TV (18), the program is interrupted with a report that your favorite charity was just given a $100,000 *grant* (Grant). Your **tub** (**19**) is filling up and overflowing with multiple *piles of hay* (Hayes).

Reread the paragraph above three times while doing your best to clearly visualize and experience everything described as if it were really happening.

You next see *Garfield the cat* (Garfield) jumping up and down on a giant **nose** (**20**) as if it were a diving board. *King Arthur* (Arthur) jumps into a large **net** (**21**) and gets all tangled up. A Catholic **nun** (**22**) has gone mad and starts running around with a *cleaver* (Cleveland). *George Harrison* (Harrison) tries to shoo off an ugly **gnome** (**23**) that is climbing all over and pestering him. **Norah** (**24**) Jones has gone mad and starts to run around with a razor-sharp *cleaver* (Cleveland again). There is a giant **nail** (**25**) going through a *Big Mac* being eaten by your *kin* (McKinley). A belt made of roses—that is, a *rose belt* (Roosevelt)—is being covered in gooey **nacho** (**26**) cheese. **Nick** (**27**) Nolte is floating in a giant cup of *tea* on a *raft* (Taft). A large **knife** (**28**) is continuously dicing a *Wilson* *tennis ball* (Wilson). You become angry and give your front door **knob** (**29**) a really *hard ding* (Harding), causing it to fall off.

Reread the paragraph above three times while doing your best to clearly visualize and experience everything described as if it were really happening.

Next, you see a **mouse** (**30**) in a *cool fridge* (Coolidge) with icicles forming on it. **Matt** (**31**) Damon is juggling a bunch of animal *hooves* (Hoover). A *rose belt* (Roosevelt) starts to wrap itself around the **moon** (**32**). Your **mom** (**33**) squeezes the biceps of a bodybuilder and calls him a *"true man"* (Truman). You watch a **mare** (**34**) continuously try to climb up an *ice tower* (Eisenhower). *JFK* (Kennedy) is opening all of his fan **mail** (**35**). A **match** (**36**) lights up under a bottle of *Johnson's* (Johnson; that is, LBJ) baby oil, causing it to splatter all over you. **Mike** (**37**) Tyson punches *Richard Nixon* (Nixon) in his nose causing it to grow out long and pointy. You see a movie (**38**) being shown on a screen set up in the back of a *Ford® pickup truck* (Ford). A **mop** (**39**) starts to mop up a *shopping cart* (Carter) until it fills up with suds. *Ronald Reagan* (Reagan) plucks the petals of a **rose** (**40**) and throws them high into the air. A large metal **rod** (**41**) starts to smash up a green *bush* (Bush). *Bill Clinton* (Clinton) plays his saxophone and dances in the **rain** (**42**). A battering **ram** (**43**) starts to batter down a giant bush (Bush). **Rory** (**44**) McIlroy is playing golf with *Barack Obama* (Obama). A dinner **roll** (**45**) spins on the head of *Donald Trump* (Trump).

Reread the paragraph above three times while doing your best to clearly visualize and experience everything described as if it were really happening.

It's test time! Write the appropriate president's surname in the spaces below. If you have difficulty with any of them, feel free to review the corresponding paragraphs above.

20th president _____

10th president _____

27th president _____

14th president _____

33rd president _____

40th president _____

7th president _____

21st president _____

12th president _____

20th president _____

Go ahead and recite all the U.S. presidents in order. Next, try it backward. In completing this chapter, you've further developed your memory skills, and have gained some valuable knowledge at the same time. It should now be clear just how powerful and useful your 00–99 images can be. I hope that you'll enjoy using them to learn as much as you can.

7

SCHOOL IS BACK IN SESSION

The techniques covered in this book can give students a huge advantage in their academic careers. These techniques can also benefit entrepreneurs and professionals who find themselves studying to earn new certifications, learn new technology, master corporate training materials, and more. Memory is fundamental to learning, so improving your ability to remember will help you to be more successful in whatever you do, whether you are a student or working professional. At some point in our lives, in one form or another, we all find ourselves with school back in session.

If you're studying for a biology exam, for example, you might need to recall that the function of the *mitochondria* is to produce energy for cells. How can you commit this fact to memory using what you've learned in previous chapters? As you've done previously, you'll want to turn what you are trying to remember into a simple image or a series of memorable images. You will also want to involve as many senses as possible and use your creativity and imagination to make what you are seeing and experiencing in your mind crazy and bizarre in some way.

PLACEHOLDER IMAGES

In addition to what you've learned in previous chapters, you'll need something new that I like to call *placeholder imagery*. Placeholder imagery consists of an image or a series of images that you will visualize and use to *temporarily* represent the word or term you're trying to memorize. Later, you'll translate that placeholder imagery back into the word or term it was meant to represent. This will all become clearer as I illustrate using mitochondria as an example.

To remember the main function of mitochondria, you'll first need to decide on some placeholder imagery to represent it. You might visualize a "mighty kite." This kite is mighty because it's covered in big muscles. This is absurd imagery, for sure, but it's memorable. Your placeholder imagery need only remind you in some way of the term or word it's meant to represent. You would have heard the word *mitochondria* over and over in class or would have read it multiple times in the course of studying your biology book. Thanks to that familiarity, an image of a *mighty kite* should be enough to trigger the word *mitochondria.*

With the simple visual of a mighty kite set in your mind, we can now use that placeholder imagery to commit the mitochondria's function to memory. The mitochondria produce energy for cells, so you might simply visualize the mighty kite producing batteries and dropping them like bombs into jail cells. You now just need to translate that memorable imagery back into what it's meant to represent. What did you just see? You just saw a mighty kite (*mitochondria*) produce batteries (*energy*) and drop them into jail cells (*cells*). In other words, the mitochondria produce energy for cells! This is an amazingly simple way to turn even complex new terms into simple and memorable imagery.

Let's continue with an example from psychology. *Classical conditioning* is a concept that you'd likely be introduced to in an introductory psychology class. To explain this concept, your instructor might talk about the famous experiment with Pavlov's dogs. This experiment involved researchers bringing out steak and presenting it to a group of dogs. When the dogs saw the steak, they would salivate. The researchers later started to ring a bell whenever they would bring out the steak. This caused the dogs to become *conditioned* over time to salivate to the sound of the bell ringing even when there was no steak. This type of conditioning is commonly known in psychology as "classical conditioning."

You may also learn about *operant conditioning* when studying psychology. Operant conditioning involves changing behavior based on experience, and often involves reward and punishment. To illustrate operant conditioning, you may read about an experiment that involved researchers putting a rat in a maze. If the rat entered the maze and took a right turn, nothing happened. However, if the rat turned left, it experienced an electric shock. The rat eventually became conditioned to always go right so as to avoid getting shocked. This is an example of operant conditioning.

When tested on operant versus classical conditioning, many students' memories will fail them and they'll mix up the two different concepts. Visualizing a simple image of a violin (*classical*) in a salivating dog's mouth would help a student avoid any confusion. It would be clear that the experiment with dogs salivating illustrated *classical* conditioning.

Next, let's tackle some terminology from astronomy. The *apogee* is the point at which an object orbiting Earth is at its *farthest* from our planet. The point at which this orbiting object is *closest* to Earth is the *perigee*. You might imagine an apple with a *G* burned into it to be your placeholder image for *apogee*. For *perigee*, you might imagine a pear with a *G* burned into it. Visualize an object of some sort continuously orbiting Earth. You see that this object is sometimes close to Earth and sometimes far from it. When the object is farthest from Earth, it instantly turns into the apple with the *G* burned into it, and when it's closest to Earth, it instantly turns into the pear with the *G* burned into it. Picturing this happening will make it easy for you to remember that when an orbiting object is closest to Earth, it's the *perigee*, and when it's farthest from Earth it's the *apogee*.

If you're taking a physics course, you will be presented with many different laws to memorize and might have difficulty remembering which law is which. *Charles's law* describes how gases tend to expand when heated. To remember this, you might visualize *Prince Charles* (a placeholder for *Charles's law*) heating up a gas can that starts to expand so that it becomes larger and larger as it's being heated. When the exam hits you with, "What law describes how gases tend to expand when heated?" you'll immediately remember the scenario with Prince Charles and the gas can. Or, if the question is simply, "What is *Charles's law*?" you can answer that it describes how a gas expands when heated. Whatever the question, the Prince Charles placeholder will make it easy for you to give the correct answer.

If you are a student studying the techniques in this book, I highly recommend taking an art history class. Art history requires a lot of memorization to prepare for exams. The famous work of art *Starry Night* was painted by Vincent van Gogh. The proper pronunciation of *van Gogh* is often debated (*Go* or *Gock*?). We'll make things easy here and go with the common American pronunciation that sounds like "van-go." Simply picture a beautiful night sky glittering with stars. Suddenly, a *van* bursts out of one of the stars. It *goes* to another star, and then *goes* to another, and so on. This scenario is your placeholder image for van Gogh. When you later need to recall who painted *Starry Night*, the image of the *van* will come to mind and remind you that it was painted by van Gogh.

What if you are taking a geography course and need to memorize countries and their corresponding capital cities? The capital of Australia is Canberra. When I hear *Australia*, the first thing that pops into my head is a *kangaroo*. A kangaroo can serve as your placeholder imagery for *Australia*. For *Canberra*, you might imagine a *tin can* with a *giant bear* on it. The kangaroo jumps onto the tin can, and somehow the giant bear magically walks out of it. When you are later asked about the capital of Australia, it will trigger the image of the kangaroo, and you'll remember that the kangaroo jumped onto the can with a giant bear on it. Thus, you'll instantly know that the capital of Australia is Canberra.

WORKING MEMORY

Let's move on to some things you might need to learn for work. If you are speaking to an audience of financial services professionals, you may want to know some financial terms—for instance, the difference between a *bull market* and a *bear market*. A financial market in which stock prices are rising or expected to rise is called a "bull market." A financial market in which stock prices are falling or expected to fall is called a "bear market." You could visualize money getting pushed *up* a hill by a *bull* (placeholder imagery for a bull market), and money getting pushed *down* a hill by a *bear* (placeholder imagery for a bear market). This should easily lock the meaning of these two financial terms into your memory.

A chart you are presented with at work depicts the past year's sources of sales and their respective percentages. The numbers break down as follows:

45% from online marketing efforts

35% from word of mouth

15% from repeat customers

5% from public relations (PR) efforts

To memorize this information, you'll need to use concepts covered in this chapter, along with the phonetic alphabet system covered in chapter 5 (page 43). You can imagine seeing a computer (placeholder imagery for online marketing) that has a gigantic roll (image for 45 percent, based on the phonetic alphabet system) coming out of it. Next, you see a large mouth (placeholder imagery for word of mouth) with mail (image for 35 percent) shooting out of it. Now, picture a bunch of people holding receipts (placeholder imagery for repeat customers), who are growing tails (image for 15 percent). Finally, visualize a stack of newspapers and magazines (placeholder for PR) with a sail (image for 5 percent) growing out of it.

Given any specific source of sales, you should now be able to easily recall the respective percentage. Thinking of repeat customers, for instance, will call to mind your placeholder imagery of people holding receipts, and you'll see them start to grow tails— so you'll realize that the correct percentage is 15 percent.

You can also memorize the above sources of sales in order, starting with the highest percentage and ending with the lowest. This can be accomplished easily, using the story method covered in chapter 1, along with the placeholder imagery you came up with for the source of sales. Picture a computer (online sales) that has a giant mouth (word of mouth) appearing on its screen. A bunch of people holding receipts (repeat customers) run out of the mouth. For some strange reason, these people are eating newspapers and magazines (PR). Replay the story in your mind and you'll easily remember the sources of sales in order of their percentages.

Let's try another example. A new product has just been released and, as a member of your company's sales and marketing team, you are charged with knowing all its benefits so you can easily discuss it with potential customers. The following benefits of the product must be committed to memory: speed, low cost, flexibility, power, and ease of use. Let's use the journey method to tackle this.

Since you have five product benefits to commit to memory, you'll need a five-location journey. Choose five locations from your office in a logical order, in which it would make sense to encounter them as you walk through your office. At your journey's first location, you see Usain Bolt running (placeholder imagery for speed). There are a few pennies spinning at your journey's second location (placeholder imagery for low cost). Gumby is wrapping himself around the third location of your journey (placeholder imagery for flexibility). At the next location of your journey, you encounter a power plant (placeholder imagery for power). A baby is playing with your company's new product at the last location of your journey (placeholder imagery for ease of use). Mentally, take a walk back through your journey. The placeholder imagery at each location will make it easy to recall all your product's benefits.

In this chapter, you've learned to combine the new concept of placeholder imagery with techniques you learned in earlier chapters. This enables you to effectively memorize a wide variety of material you could encounter at school or work. Although it's impossible to cover every possible exam scenario in this book, with a little creative tweaking of what you've learned here, you can easily remember just about anything at all!

8

LANGUAGES OF THE WORLD

One of my favorite applications for the techniques in this book is memorizing new foreign language vocabulary. In this chapter, I'll focus primarily on Korean words. What you'll learn here, however, will serve you well when studying just about *any* new language. The goal is to develop a skill set that you can later apply to many different situations.

There are three main parts to learning a foreign language: understanding the rules of grammar, building up your vocabulary, and refining your pronunciation. Building your vocabulary tends to take the most time when studying a new language, because without training it's difficult to memorize foreign words and their meanings. Luckily, of the three main parts to learning a new language, building up your vocabulary is the one I can help you with the most, given what you've learned so far in this book. It should be fairly easy for you to learn a hundred new words a day in a foreign language if you are dedicated and correctly apply the methodology in this chapter. The icing on the cake is that, unlike with traditional methods of rote memorization, the process that I'll teach you is a lot of fun!

OF MONSTERS AND BEANS

To illustrate how the process works, let's go over some Korean words. The Korean equivalent for the English word *bean* is *kong*. Visualize a giant green bean. King Kong suddenly comes along and starts to eat the bean quickly and messily, causing pieces of it to fly everywhere. When you later try to remember the Korean word for *bean*, the image of King Kong eating the bean will come back to you and remind you that the word you want to use is *kong*. It doesn't matter if the pronunciation of the Korean word *kong* does not sound exactly like the *Kong* in *King Kong*. You'll likely have heard the new words you're trying to learn many times, either from an instructor, a CD or a DVD, or an online recording. So, as long as an image of King Kong is enough to remind you of the word *kong*, you will be fine, even if the words are not pronounced exactly the same. The imagery you create serves as a mental "cue card" to help you call to mind the correct word.

With the example of *bean* above, a single image of King Kong is adequate to remind us of the Korean word *kong*. However, other scenarios may require a series of images to bring to mind the correct foreign word. You'll see this in the next example.

The Korean word for *water* is *mul*. When spoken aloud, the word *mul* sounds a bit like "moo-l." Visualize a giant pool of water. A cow now jumps into this pool of water and starts to swim around. Thus, the pool of water is now a "moo-l" of water, since a cow says "moo"! This funny series of images will help tremendously. When you later need to remember the Korean word for *water*, the imagery of the pool that turns into a "moo-l" will come back to you and thus remind you that the correct word is *mul*.

Here are a few more examples:

The Korean word for *chicken* is *dalg*, which sounds sort of like *tack* when spoken. Visualize a chicken getting impaled by a giant tack. This will cue up the memory of *dalg* when you need to recall the Korean word for *chicken*.

Ppang is the Korean word for *bread*. When spoken aloud it sounds sort of like *bang* in English. Picture a loaf of bread that fires off like a rifle with a loud bang!

The Korean word for *rice* is *bap*. When spoken aloud, the Korean word *bap* sounds similar to the English word *bop*. Imagine that you are eating a bowl of rice and it starts to pop like popcorn and bop you in the head.

Coffee in Korean is *keopi*, which sounds similar to the English word *copy* when spoken aloud. Imagine that you place a cup of coffee on top of a copy machine and hit the START button. The machine then begins to magically pump out real cups of coffee.

House in Korean is *jib*, which sounds similar to *jeep* in English. Visualize your house being carted off by a jeep!

The Korean for *sugar* is *seoltang*, which sounds like *soul-tongue* in English when spoken aloud. Picture a large box of sugar. A ghostlike figure (a soul) rises out of the box and starts to wiggle its giant tongue. This imagery represents "soul-tongue."

MEMORIZING SYLLABLES

When memorizing foreign words using this process, I recommend deciding on images that will represent certain common syllables that words may contain at their beginning, middle, or end. Apples might remind you of the syllable *a*, which sounds like "uh." Apples might be used simply because the word *apples* begins with the letter *a*. A hula hoop, which has an *o*-shape, might remind you of the syllable *o*, which sounds like "oh." There are different ways to go about deciding on your images. Just be sure they each in some way remind you of the syllable they're meant to represent.

Let's go over a couple of examples of how to use images for syllables when studying foreign languages. These examples will use Spanish words. The Spanish word for *chair* is *silla*, which sounds like "sea-uh" in English when spoken aloud. Simply picture a chair. This chair is floating in the sea and getting smashed by the waves. Suddenly, apples start to fly out of the chair. Later, when you need to recall the Spanish word for *chair*, first the sea will pop into your head (*sea*) and then the apples (*uh*). This combined imagery will get you to *silla* ("sea-uh"). *Tio* is the Spanish word for *uncle* and sounds like "tea-oh" in English when spoken aloud. Visualize your uncle drinking a cup of tea (*tea*) that has a hula hoop (*oh*) coming out of it. This will get you to *tio* ("tea-oh") when you need to say *uncle* in Spanish.

Review the chart below a couple of times before continuing.

English Word	Foreign Word	Approximate Pronunciation	Imagery
bean	kong	"koh-ong"	King Kong is eating a bean
water	mul	"moo-l"	A cow swimming in a pool of water
chicken	dalg	"tack"	A chicken being impaled by a tack
bread	ppang	"bang"	A loaf of bread fires off like a rifle with a bang
rice	bap	"bop"	A bowl of rice starts to pop and bop you in the head
coffee	keopi	"copy"	A copy machine starts to copy some coffee

English Word	Foreign Word	Approximate Pronunciation	Imagery
house	jib	"jeep"	Your house is being carted off by a jeep
sugar	seoltang	"soul-tongue"	A soul wiggling a tongue rises from a box of sugar
chair	silla	"sea-uh"	A chair broken up by the sea with apples flying
uncle	tio	"tea-oh"	Your uncle drinking a cup of tea with a hula hoop

Next, try to complete the chart below. For each foreign word, fill in the English equivalent:

Foreign Word	English Word
kong	
mul	
dalg	
ppang	
bap	
keopi	
jib	
seoltang	
silla	
tio	

Since you have created intertwining images, it's easy to remember the foreign word if you're given its English equivalent and vice versa. When you hear someone say one of the words you've been studying, you'll likely understand what is being said, thanks to your imagery cuing up the memory of the English equivalent.

What you've learned in this chapter probably isn't enough to become *fluent* in a foreign language. However, you'll be able to rapidly learn new vocabulary words and short phrases. This will give you a huge advantage when studying a new language or learning a few key words when traveling. Any effort on your part to say even a few words or phrases in the native tongue of someone you're interacting with can help build rapport. Your effort will always be appreciated. I love to memorize short phrase books when I'm on my way to give a speech in a country where English isn't the primary language. It helps me to build better relationships with people attending my presentations. When drinking tea in Korea, it isn't necessary to say, "Can I get some sugar, please?" Just say *seoltang?* with an interrogative tone of voice. Don't underestimate the power of learning a few key words and phrases.

Now, get out there and conquer the world!

9

LET'S PLAY CARDS!

When people hear that I'm a memory champion, it's common for them to say to me, "Let's go to Vegas!" Card counting in blackjack has more to do with math than memory and involves keeping a running "count" that's adjusted according to which cards are dealt. However, there *are* card games, such as bridge, in which having a great memory can be a huge asset. Moreover, memorizing decks of playing cards is a great way to practice the techniques in this book, and is excellent exercise for your memory.

Memorizing the order of all fifty-two playing cards in a freshly shuffled deck might seem like an impossible task to some people. Believe it or not, though, it's much easier than it might seem at first. When I was at the top of my game, I could do it in less than ninety seconds. In this chapter, I will teach you exactly how I did it. You'll soon amaze yourself, your family, and your friends with this incredible feat!

WHEN A SPADE'S NOT A SPADE

At this point, you already have most of the tools you need to memorize a deck of playing cards. We'll be using the journey method, along with the phonetic alphabet system. The phonetic alphabet system will help you come up with an image that you can visualize for each playing card. Then, it's just a matter of linking the images together along a journey to memorize the cards in order.

My image for the ace of spades is *suit*. How did I come up with *suit* for the ace of spades? Since *spades* begins with the *s*-sound, our corresponding word should also begin with the *s*-sound. The ending consonant sound for our corresponding word comes from the rank of the playing card and the phonetic alphabet system. Aces have a rank of 1, so our word must end with either the *t*- or *d*-sound, since those sounds correspond to the number 1 in the phonetic alphabet system.

Vowel sounds can be added anywhere to help form words for playing cards. In this case, I inserted the *oo*-sound and came up with the word *suit*. Once more, the *s* in *suit* comes from *spades* and the *t* comes from the ace's rank of 1. My image for the 2 of spades is the yellow *sun*. The *s* in *sun* comes from *spades*, and the *n* comes from the rank of 2. Remember that in the phonetic alphabet system, the sound corresponding to the number 2 is *n*.

Keeping the two examples above in mind, review the following playing card–word pairs on the next page.

Only the 0 from the number 10 will be used for cards with a rank of 10. Ignoring the 1, words for cards with a rank of 10 should end with the *s*- or *z*-sound, per the sounds corresponding to 0 in the phonetic alphabet system. Therefore, the 10 of spades is represented by *sauce*. The words for all the jacks in a deck are the same as the suit for that specific jack. Therefore, the word for the jack of spades is simply *spade*. The jack of hearts, of course, would then be *heart*.

The queens and kings in the deck are represented by queens and kings from history or pop culture that we can in some way associate with the respective suit. For the queen and king of spades, we'll focus on color to make our association. Spades are black, so a *queen bee* will represent the queen of spades, since black rings swirl around the body of a queen bee. *King Kong* will represent the king of spades, since King Kong has black fur.

Below is a list of all playing cards in a standard fifty-two-card deck and words that I recommend to represent them. The purpose of the words is to help you produce a corresponding *image* in your mind. It won't happen right away, but, with practice, eventually when you a see a playing card, the image representing it will pop into your head without your even thinking of the word. This will take time, but it will start to happen with consistent training.

ace of spades = suit	**8 of spades = safe**
2 of spades = sun	**9 of spades = soap**
3 of spades = Sam (Uncle)	**10 of spades = sauce**
4 of spades = sore	**jack of spades = spade**
5 of spades = soil	**queen of spades = queen bee**
6 of spades = sash	**king of spades = King Kong**
7 of spades = sock	

ace of hearts = hat

2 of hearts = Han (Solo)

3 of hearts = ham

4 of hearts = hair

5 of hearts = hail

6 of hearts = hash

7 of hearts = hook

8 of hearts = hoof

9 of hearts = hoop

10 of hearts = hose

jack of hearts = heart

queen of hearts = Dairy Queen (think "people love ice cream"; love = heart)

king of hearts = Burger King (think "people love hamburgers"; love = heart)

ace of diamonds = date

2 of diamonds = Dan (Aykroyd)

3 of diamonds = dam

4 of diamonds = door

5 of diamonds = doll

6 of diamonds = dish

7 of diamonds = duck

8 of diamonds = dove

9 of diamonds = dip

10 of diamonds = dice

jack of diamonds = diamond

queen of diamonds = Queen Elizabeth (might own a lot of diamonds)

king of diamonds = King Tut (might have been buried with diamonds)

ace of clubs = cat	9 of clubs = cup
2 of clubs = cane	10 of clubs = case
3 of clubs = comb	jack of clubs = club
4 of clubs = car	queen of clubs = Queen Latifah (her music might be played in a dance club)
5 of clubs = coal	
6 of clubs = cash	king of clubs = King of Pop, Michael Jackson (his music might be played in a dance club)
7 of clubs = cake	
8 of clubs = cave	

Review the word-image pairs for each card. Go ahead and change any of the words if you feel that another word would work better for you personally. However, once you choose a word, I advise you to stick to it and not change it in the future. Again, the *images* are what we want eventually popping into your head, not the *words*. This level of fluency can only be achieved if you see the same image in your head each and every time. When you are comfortable with your image for each card, you can move on to memorizing the playing cards in order.

TIP While at first you'll need to learn the word for each playing card, the goal is to have an image instantly pop into your head upon seeing any card.

PLAYING WITH HALF A DECK

Since it will take some time and practice to comfortably memorize an entire fifty-two-card deck, I'm going to illustrate the process with a half deck (twenty-six cards). I advise people to begin memorizing half decks for practice and then later move on to an entire deck, after memorizing twenty-six cards becomes easy for you. We are going to put two images at each location of a journey, so for twenty-six cards (half a deck), we'll need a thirteen-location journey (13 × 2 = 26). In chapter 2, you learned the types of locations that work well with the journey method.

Choose your thirteen locations now. Make sure that you can mentally traverse all thirteen locations in order from memory before you proceed to the next paragraph. Once you have your thirteen-location journey ready, we will use it to memorize the following twenty-six playing cards in order: 7 of hearts, 4 of spades, 9 of clubs, 3 of hearts, 10 of clubs, king of clubs, 10 of diamonds, 2 of hearts, 6 of clubs, 4 of diamonds, queen of hearts, 10 of hearts, 3 of clubs, jack of diamonds, ace of hearts, 7 of spades, ace of spades, 9 of hearts, 2 of clubs, jack of hearts, 3 of spades, 5 of spades, 4 of hearts, 9 of spades, 7 of diamonds, and 5 of clubs.

Visualize a giant **hook** at the first location of your journey. Falling onto the hook so that it gets impaled is a large ugly **sore**. Moving on to the second location of your journey, you see a gigantic **cup**, which starts overflowing with piles of **ham**. There's a giant **case** at the next location of your journey. The case bursts open and **Michael Jackson** jumps out! **Dice** are magically rolling around at your journey's subsequent location. **Han** (Solo) picks up the dice and starts to eat them. The next location of your journey is covered with a pile of **cash**. Rising out of the cash is a large, colorful **door**. You see a bunch of food from **Dairy Queen** at the next location of your journey. Suddenly, a **hose** starts to spray water all over the Dairy Queen food. There is a large black **comb** at the next location of your journey. It starts to comb through a pile

TIP You'll find that you automatically know which card comes first when you place two images at a location and see them interact together in a story. This is because, as mentioned earlier, your brain knows the order of stories you've seen, experienced, or created in your mind. If you experience any difficulty recalling the order of images, just use a simple scheme of left to right, bottom to top, top to bottom, and so on—whatever makes the most sense to you.

of **diamonds**. A huge fedora **hat** appears at your journey's next stop. **Socks** start to shoot out of the hat. You see a fancy **suit** at the subsequent location of your journey. This suit suddenly flies through a colorful **hoop**! At the next location of your journey, a large **cane** shows up. This cane is smashing up a **heart**! You see good old Uncle **Sam** at your journey's next location. Uncle Sam starts to eat some **soil**. There is a big pile of **hair** at your journey's next stop. The hair starts to get covered in **soap**. At your journey's last location, you see a giant **duck**. This duck starts to eat a bunch of **coal**.

Reread the paragraph above a couple more times while relaxing and doing your best to vividly experience all the scenarios happening at each location of your journey. You can then recall all twenty-six playing cards in order by simply taking a mental stroll through your journey. The images at each location just need to be translated back into their corresponding playing cards. Amazing, isn't it?

I encourage you to memorize a half deck of playing cards at least once a week. As you become more experienced, this will take you less and less time to accomplish. Once you are able to memorize a half deck of cards comfortably in less than ten minutes, I would recommend moving on to trying out a full deck. To do this, you'll follow the same process outlined in this chapter, but your journey will consist of twenty-six locations, since there are fifty-two cards in a full deck, with two images at each location. With consistent practice, soon you'll be memorizing entire decks of playing cards in minutes! This skill will give you an edge in many card games and is wonderful exercise for your brain.

10

THE FINAL TOUCHES

At this point, you have already begun to develop skills that will benefit you in multiple areas of your life. At the core of *all* the techniques covered in this book are the three main principles introduced in chapter 1: turning what you'd like to remember into an image or a series of images; involving as many senses as possible, thereby building more connections to help you later retrieve the information; and making these mental images as crazy and unusual as possible, allowing you to tap into the powerful *psychological* aspect of human memory.

In this chapter, it's my aim to give you some additional advice and considerations to help you refine and fine-tune these skills, which are so essential to mastering the art of committing anything at all to memory. And, since I strongly believe in the principle that a healthy body equals a healthy mind, in addition to tips related to memory techniques, I'll also include some suggested guidelines for diet and exercise.

BETTER IMAGERY, BETTER MEMORY

When it comes to applying memory techniques, not all images are the same. The following tips will help you create more effective and memorable imagery.

KING KONG AND GODZILLA

You've probably noticed in previous chapters that I often used *gigantic* or *giant* to describe various objects. Is it easier to remember seeing an ordinary bird or a gigantic bird the size of King Kong? Conjuring up images larger than they could ever possibly be in real life makes your imagery more memorable.

MORE IS OFTEN BETTER

Visualizing hundreds and thousands of something is more memorable than a lone object. Are you more likely to remember one ball hitting a car, or thousands of balls hitting it all at once?

MAKE IT COLORFUL

The more colorful the image, the better. A bright-red bird will likely stick in your memory much better than a gray one will. Also, experiment with using different colors than you'd expect to see in real life. An orange-and-green zebra will be much more memorable to you than the ordinary black-and-white variety.

ACTION!

Static imagery is not as memorable as action-packed imagery. It's much easier to remember a man doing a crazy dance or jumping jacks than a man just standing around doing nothing. Try to come up with scenarios that involve as much action as possible.

IT'S MAGIC

Imagine objects doing things they could only do with magic. Visualizing a knife cutting an apple in half won't stick in your mind the way seeing a knife cutting a steel safe in half will. Add some magic to your imagery and you'll remember more than ever.

LONG-TERM RELATIONSHIPS

I've been an international speaker on the topic of memory skills for a decade now, and one of the most common questions I receive from audiences is something like this: "Are these techniques only good for short-term memory?" Absolutely not! Everything you've learned in this book will help you take information along the path of working memory (a few seconds or less) to short-term memory (minutes, hours, or days) and eventually long-term memory (weeks, months, or years). (Note that these definitions don't exactly match what you'll find in psychology books regarding stages of memory, but they describe stages to which I feel people can best relate.)

Using the techniques you've learned so far will automatically keep information in your memory much longer than it would otherwise remain with traditional and ineffective methods of memorization such as *brute force repetition*. However, when attempting to memorize information you'd like to know long term, you'll ideally want to combine the techniques you've learned so far with a method of review that studies have shown to be effective for committing information to long-term memory. This special method is known as *spaced repetition*. Rather than reviewing a piece of information five times in one day, it's much more effective for long-term memory if you space out those five reviews over a longer time interval.

> **TIP** Certain software programs, designed around the concept of spaced repetition, are meant to help you optimize the timing of each review. You may want to check out some of them, such as CleverDeck (http://cleverdeck.com), and see if you find them useful.

Below, I've included a spaced-repetition schedule that I've personally found useful for locking information into my long-term memory:

1. My first review is done just before I go to sleep on the day I start to learn the information. One theory as to why humans sleep is that we use the time asleep to consolidate and process information we encounter while awake. Many studies have shown that reviewing information soon before falling asleep helps to embed that information in our memories. Reviewing information right before going to sleep may tell your brain that the information is important, so your brain will better process it and lock it in.

2. I always do my second review early the next morning. It's easy to quickly run through my mental images while showering or doing my morning workout.

3. My third review is usually done one week later. After completing the first two reviews, I should still remember the information in a week, although I might be on the verge of forgetting it.

4. I do my fourth review two weeks after completion of the third review. At this point, I'm already starting to know the information well.

5. My final review comes four weeks after the fourth review. After this review, the information is usually stored in my long-term memory and I'm able to recall it easily even months later. With an additional review months later, I might even remember the information for years.

The review schedule outlined here incorporates the concept of spaced repetition and works well for me. However, I recommend that you treat it only as a guideline. The most effective schedule will be different for each individual, and will also depend on what you are trying to commit to memory. It's probably best to start out with the five reviews that I've outlined, and then make adjustments as you discover what works best for you.

Another principle that I recommend applying is a technique often referred to as *active recall*. With active recall, you *actively* make an effort to recall something you've attempted to commit to memory. Believe it or not, a lot of people never take this important step when trying to memorize information. It's common for people to simply read the information over and over again until they *think* it has sunk into their memory, but they never test themselves to see if they are able to recall it. Self-testing is an effective way to employ the principle of active recall. Earlier, you memorized a long list of Academy Award winners for Best Picture. Reading the list many times or repeatedly reviewing your imagery without performing any sort of self-test would be considered only *passive* reviewing. Challenging yourself to write down the winners from memory on a sheet of paper or to recite them orally without error would be an act of *active* recall. For information you need to know long term, I advise you to combine visual-based techniques from earlier chapters with self-testing for active recall. This powerful combination will lock information into your mind for easy recall when you need it.

MEMORY BOOSTERS

You're no doubt familiar with this popular saying: "You are what you eat." When you're setting out to improve your memory, diet is something important to take into consideration. Our bodies need certain essential vitamins and minerals to function properly. If you aren't getting the recommended dietary allowance (RDA) of essential vitamins and minerals through the food you eat (preferably from natural food sources), it may be a good idea to try taking a daily multivitamin to compensate for what you might be lacking in your diet. There is a lot of research to support the notion that a healthy body equals a healthy mind. In terms of supporting memory function specifically, I recommend consulting your doctor to make sure that you get enough omega-3 fatty acids (essential for normal brain function) and B-vitamins (needed for mental energy and concentration).

Exercise is another important consideration when trying to strengthen your memory and keep it sharp. Regular exercise is a factor in keeping your body healthy, so it follows that it will have an impact on your mind as well. Blood flow to the brain is increased with exercise. This helps to keep your brain oxygenated and improves its performance. In addition, there has been some fascinating research on how being physically active while studying can improve learning. I had the honor of speaking at a TED conference with many world-renowned experts on memory. My favorite talk, given by Dr. Wendy Suzuki from New York University, was about the impact of exercise on learning and memory. Dr. Suzuki recommends moving around while learning, something that has always worked for me. I highly recommend checking out some of her research. If you're serious about improving your memory, talk to your physician about weekly exercise that might be appropriate for you. It won't necessarily take a lot to have a positive impact. Consistency is the key!

MEMORY KILLERS

I'd like to conclude this chapter by briefly going over three of the top killers of memory. One is excess intake of alcohol. Drinking too much on a regular basis will eventually have a long-term negative impact on your memory. Alcohol impairs the encoding of new memories and can cause permanent damage to memory cells if abused over a long period.

Another top memory killer is lack of sleep. A few nights of not getting enough rest might not hurt your memory too badly, but if you're consistently failing to get the sleep your brain needs to fully recover each day, you will start to find it difficult to remember things.

The third memory killer to avoid is too much stress. We are all faced with stressful situations at one point or another. This is perfectly normal. However, if you are constantly stressed out over the course of weeks or months, it's inevitable that you'll start to experience memory problems.

Armed with the memory-building techniques you've learned throughout this book, and the additional tips and considerations from this chapter, you now have all the tools you need to develop a truly superpowered memory. It's well within your reach.

11

THE USA MEMORY CHAMPIONSHIP

Once you've read all the chapters in this book and have
completed all the exercises and advanced challenges found in
the workbook section that follows, you will have developed the
skills necessary to compete in the USA Memory Championship.
The championship was created in 1997 by Tony Dottino and
Marshall Tarley, and is usually held in the Northeast. It has received
a tremendous amount of media attention over the years and is
often televised on cable television. During this one-day, annual
competition, contestants from around the country compete in the
memorization of hundreds of names, numbers, lines of poetry,
playing cards, words, and much more. There are seven events in
all. In the first four written qualifying events, each person competes
individually in silence. The last three championship events are held
onstage in front of a large audience and the media. On the next
page is an outline of the various events and how you can prepare
for each one.

NAMES AND FACES

The first event is Names and Faces. You are given thirteen sheets of paper, each with photos of 9 different people on it, so the total number of people on the sheets is 117 (13 × 9). Written below each photo is the person's first and last name. You are given fifteen minutes to study all thirteen sheets. When the fifteen-minute memorization period is up, the sheets are immediately taken away. At that point, you'll be handed thirteen new sheets with all 117 photos on them; however, the photos will be in a completely different order without the names written underneath. Your task will be to write down from memory each person's first and/or last name under his or her photo. You earn one point for each correct first name, and another point for each correct last name. It's important to note that spelling counts! If you spell a name incorrectly, you will not be awarded a point for remembering that name, even if you're close. The recall period you're allotted for this event is twenty minutes. A competitive score is seventy-five or more names correctly remembered.

To prepare to compete in this event, you need to master the techniques you learned in chapter 4 of this book. Along with practicing with people you meet in real life, I recommend using LinkedIn and social media sites. Both will provide you with photos and corresponding names with which to practice. I also have an online course with photos you can check out on my website (www. internationalmanofmemory.com).

SPEED NUMBERS

The second event is Speed Numbers. In this event, you are given a sheet of computer-generated random digits and tasked with perfectly memorizing the longest sequence you can in five minutes. There are twenty digits in each row and twenty-five rows on the page. You cannot skip a row when memorizing. After you study the digits for five minutes, the sheet is taken away and you are given a blank sheet on which to write the sequences from memory. You must write out each row of digits from memory in the same order presented on the first sheet (the memorization sheet). For each row of digits that you correctly write out from memory, you are awarded twenty points. Any row with even a single error results in no points awarded for that row. You are given two separate trials (two memorization and recall periods) for this event, and only the higher score is counted. A competitive score in this event is a sequence eighty digits or longer perfectly memorized in five minutes.

To prepare for this event, you'll need to master the phonetic alphabet system covered in chapter 5, beginning on page 43, as well as the preset images for the number sequences 00–99 covered in chapter 6, beginning on page 58. I'd recommend combining the principles covered in those chapters with the journey method. A good starting strategy would be to place a couple of two-digit images at each location of your journey as you memorize the long number sequences. This will have you memorizing four digits at a time. If you mentally populate a twenty-five-location journey while memorizing, you will have committed a one-hundred-digit sequence to memory (25 locations × 4 digits at each location). To practice for this event, you can take advantage of a number of online random-number generators. Just make sure that each row consists of twenty random digits, so your practice is consistent with what you'll tackle in the actual competition. You can also set up an Excel spreadsheet to accomplish this.

SPEED CARDS

The third competition event is Speed Cards. For this event you are given a shuffled deck of playing cards and must memorize the exact order of all fifty-two cards in five minutes or less. If more than one person successfully memorizes the entire deck, the fastest time wins. The first time you compete in this event, I recommend that you just try to memorize the entire deck in five minutes. I wouldn't worry about trying for a faster time. There are two trials for this event, though, with the better score counting. So if you are able to memorize the deck perfectly in five minutes in the first trial, at that point go ahead and try for a faster time in the second trial.

This is one of the more popular events for spectators to watch because of the way it's scored. After the memorization period is complete, competitors are then given another deck of cards (the recall deck) in a new order. Your task is to arrange the second deck from memory into the same order as the first. You have a maximum of five minutes to do so. The two decks are then placed side by side, and one card from each deck is flipped at a time to make sure all the cards match. Scoring stops when there is a discrepancy between the two decks. So, if the first fourteen cards of each deck match, but the fifteenth card in one deck is different from the fifteenth card in the other, scoring stops and a score of fourteen cards is awarded.

To be competitive in this event, you'll need to be able to memorize all fifty-two cards in order in five minutes. Chapter 9 describes everything you need to do well in this Speed Cards event. To practice, simply shuffle a deck of cards and test yourself on memorizing the cards, in order, as fast as you can. It's easy and fun to practice for this event on a regular basis.

POETRY

The fourth event in the championship is Poetry. A fifty-line poem is written specifically for the event so that there's no chance anyone has seen it before. Competitors are given fifteen minutes to memorize the poem line by line and word for word. In addition to memorizing each line of the poem word for word, competitors must also indicate in their recall every instance of a capital letter, punctuation mark, and word placed in bold or italics. After the fifteen-minute memorization period is complete, the poem is taken away and competitors are given blank sheets of paper on which to rewrite the poem. For every line that is recalled 100 percent accurately, competitors are awarded one point for every word, capital letter, punctuation mark, and instance of words in bold or italics. If there is a single mistake on a line, zero points are awarded for that line. The points for each line are added up, yielding a grand total for the entire poem. A competitive score in this event is somewhere around one hundred points.

To prepare for this event, you'll need to master all the material covered in chapter 2. The same methodology for memorizing a speech applies to memorizing a poem. You may need to make your imagery even more detailed so you can memorize every word. A great way to practice for this event is to regularly memorize poems from the Poetry.com website.

The four events reviewed above are the qualifying events, in which all entered competitors must compete. The results from each qualifying event are tallied together to compute an overall score and ranking for each competitor. The top eight ranked competitors advance to the final three championship rounds. The remaining competitors are eliminated from the competition.

SPOKEN WORDS

The first championship round is called Spoken Words. For this event, the eight finalists are taken to a back room, where they are given fifteen minutes to memorize two hundred random words in order. You don't necessarily need to memorize all two hundred words to make it past this round. You can attempt as many of the two hundred as you'd like, but the words must be memorized consecutively and in the exact order given on the memorization sheet. There's a bit of strategy involved with this event. I'd advise you to memorize only the number of consecutive words that you are certain you'll be able to recite in order from memory. This is because of how this event is scored. Once the fifteen-minute memorization period is up, the eight finalists are brought out from the back room and onto a stage in front of hundreds of spectators and representatives from the media. The first competitor must correctly recite the first word from memory, the second competitor must correctly recite the second word from memory, the third competitor must give the third word, and so on. If it's your turn to recite the next word and you either give the wrong word or fail to recite a word within fifteen seconds, you are immediately eliminated from the competition. Yes, this is a single-elimination round. In other words, just one mistake and you're out! This round will continue until three finalists are eliminated, leaving only five remaining.

To prepare for this event, I recommend that you practice memorizing random word lists from the internet. You can use either the story method or the journey method to memorize the random words in order. I know competitors who have been successful with both techniques, but I personally would recommend using the journey method.

THREE STRIKES YOU'RE OUT

The remaining five finalists compete in the Three Strikes You're Out (also known as the Tea Party) event. In this event, the five finalists are given fifteen minutes to hear and review facts about six strangers. Six people come onstage, one at a time, and give their name (first, middle, and last), birth date (month, day, and year), address (city, state, and zip code), phone number (seven-digit number), pet (name, type, and color), three favorite hobbies, favorite car (year, make/model, and color), and three favorite foods. This oral recitation is supposed to take about 7½ minutes of the memorization period. The remaining 7½ minutes of the memorization period can be used by the finalists to review the facts about each person on information sheets handed out to each finalist. Once the entire fifteen-minute memorization period is up, the finalists are randomly quizzed on the facts about all six people. If a competitor fails to recall any piece of information he or she is asked—i.e., stranger #4's birth date—that competitor is immediately given a strike. If a competitor accumulates three strikes, he or she is immediately eliminated from the competition. This round continues until two more finalists are eliminated, leaving only three remaining.

Preparing to compete in this particular event can be rather difficult. It would probably be best to have someone create data sheets for you that contain facts about invented people. I'd recommend using the journey method for this, so you'd need six journeys for six different people. Each journey will consist of eight locations, since there are eight different facts you need to know about each person.

DOUBLE DECK O'CARDS

The three remaining finalists then compete in the final event of the competition: Double Deck O'Cards. For this event, the finalists are tasked with memorizing the exact order of two separate shuffled decks of playing cards in five minutes. The exact order of all 104 cards (52 cards × 2 decks) must be memorized within five minutes. The decks are designated as deck #1 and deck #2. Memorization must begin with the first deck and then continue with the second. Once the five-minute memorization period concludes, the first competitor recites the first card from deck #1, the second competitor the second card from deck #1, the third competitor the third card from deck #1, then back to the first competitor for the fourth card from deck #1, and so on. Once the first deck is recalled, the recall period continues with the second deck. If it's your turn to recite the next card and you either give the wrong card or fail to recite a card within fifteen seconds, you are immediately eliminated from the competition. This round eliminates two more finalists, leaving only one finalist, who is then crowned the USA National Memory Champion!

I hope this book has awakened you to the world of improved memory and inspired you to someday try to compete in this amazing annual competition. Again, if you've completed the exercises and challenges in this book, you have the necessary skills. I'm sure that you'll cherish the unique and exciting experience of competing in a national championship with a large audience and abundant media attention. (Go to www.usamemorychampionship. com for more information.) However, and more importantly, preparing to compete in the USA Memory Championship will help you sharpen and hone incredibly valuable memory skills that will benefit you in multiple areas of your life.

MEMORY
WORKBOOK

PRACTICE MAKES PERFECT!

Like any other skill you might hope to develop—such as golf,
piano, crochet, or juggling—consistent *practice* is necessary for you
to master your ability to remember.

This workbook section will provide you with fun exercises and
challenges to attempt. If you follow through and complete these
exercises, I'm confident you'll realize you have developed a valuable
skill that will benefit you for the rest of your life. If you prefer not
to write in this book, feel free, of course, to list your answers on
separate sheets of paper.

Let's get started!

EXERCISES

Please use the *story method* to memorize the following random word list:

disco	bandanna	moon
coin	photograph	triangle
giraffe	movie	ocean
spaghetti	quilt	tortilla
zebra	belt	library
desk	zoo	dragon
suitcase	dessert	

Test your recall by filling in the blanks below:

_____   _____

_____   _____

_____   _____

_____   _____

_____   _____

_____   _____

_____   _____

_____   _____

_____   _____

Let's try another exercise with the *story method*. This word list contains some words that are more abstract than simple nouns. You can do this! The key is to create images that will in some way remind you of each word as you develop the story. Here is the list:

time	**clarity**	**happy**
joy	**eternity**	**rest**
consistent	**distance**	**holiday**
truth	**attain**	**elevate**
engage	**elegant**	**commerce**
creativity	**cold**	**expensive**
persevere	**love**	

Test your recall by filling in the blanks below:

_____   _____

_____   _____

_____   _____

_____   _____

_____   _____

_____   _____

_____   _____

_____   _____

_____   _____

_____   _____

Instead of twenty random words, you'll now attempt to memorize eighteen random names. Again, please use the *story method*. This exercise will serve as good practice in creating images to remind you of the names of people you meet.

Jim	**Nick**	**Harry**
Jacob	**Ted**	**Crystal**
Shannon	**Marshall**	**Kim**
Clarice	**Jed**	**Emilia**
Debra	**Lily**	**Derek**
Bill	**Angela**	**Peggy**

Test your recall by filling in the blanks below:

_____   _____

_____   _____

_____   _____

_____   _____

_____   _____

_____   _____

_____   _____

_____   _____

_____   _____

Next up is an exercise similar to the one above; however, this time some of the names won't be typical Western names you may be more used to encountering. To effectively tackle this challenge, you may need to come up with a series of images to remind you of each name as you create your story. It might be useful to break some names down by syllable. For example, you might remember the name *Benjawan* by visualizing a banjo (*Benja-*) played by a wand (*wan*). Here's the list:

Benjawan	**Nikola**	**Sanjiv**	**Alena**
Rodolfo	**Zeynep**	**Samia**	**Quinn**
Tak	**Alana**	**Niraj**	**Pedro**
Ursula	**Karolina**	**Bianca**	**Bernie**
Rushmi	**Sumit**	**Payton**	**Yulian**

Test your recall by filling in the blanks below:

_____   _____

_____   _____

_____   _____

_____   _____

_____   _____

_____   _____

_____   _____

_____   _____

_____   _____

_____   _____

Next, use the *journey method* to memorize the following random word list. There are twenty words, so you'll need a journey consisting of twenty locations. Here's the list:

burrito	**bag**	**tea**
marker	**sandwich**	**circus**
lion	**club**	**sea**
cradle	**monkey**	**thread**
diamond	**cabin**	**shirt**
fur	**rose**	**fire**
resort	**ship**	

Test your recall by filling in the blanks below:

_____   _____

_____   _____

_____   _____

_____   _____

_____   _____

_____   _____

_____   _____

_____   _____

_____   _____

_____   _____

I'd like you to use the *journey method* again, but this time for a list of words that are more abstract. Once again there are twenty words, so you'll need a journey consisting of twenty locations. Here's the new list:

best	**courage**	**treatment**
remarkable	**health**	**circumstance**
lie	**ready**	**graduate**
crime	**lean**	**wizard**
diet	**hero**	**age**
ferocious	**justice**	**apply**
red	**shape**	

Test your recall by filling in the blanks below:

_____   _____

_____   _____

_____   _____

_____   _____

_____   _____

_____   _____

_____   _____

_____   _____

_____   _____

_____   _____

This exercise will give you more practice with the *phonetic alphabet system*. Below are some random items and a corresponding count for each one—for instance, 15 rackets. This example could be committed to memory by imagining a *racket* growing a large *tail* (15). Here we go:

15 rackets	**38 pencils**	**49 cards**
25 goblins	**30 women**	**41 stones**
99 geese	**27 masks**	**70 blankets**
45 envelopes	**95 sweaters**	**68 otters**
11 jackets	**62 castles**	**42 wagons**
57 wolves	**18 turkeys**	**90 doctors**
65 dragons	**74 phones**	

Test your recall by filling in the blanks below:

90	_____	25	_____
41	_____	42	_____
11	_____	57	_____
65	_____	30	_____
38	_____	27	_____
95	_____	62	_____
18	_____	70	_____
68	_____	99	_____
74	_____	49	_____
45	_____	15	_____

CHALLENGES

I now challenge you to complete the four exercises below, each of which offers benefits for your personal life.

1. Memorize your driver's license number. Hint: Use the story method and begin your story with an image of a car or a generic-looking license. For any letters, simply use an image corresponding to a word that begins with that letter. If your license contains an A, you might use an apple; for B, you might use a butterfly; and so on.

2. If you have a passport, memorize your passport number. Hint: Use the same process as with the previous challenge, but begin your story with an image of your passport booklet.

3. Memorize all your credit card numbers, along with the expiration dates and security codes. Hint: You could either use the journey method here, creating a different journey for each card, or the story method, beginning a unique story for each card with an image that will remind you of it. For example, a Discover® card could be represented by a disc, and an American Express® card could be represented by an American flag.

4. Memorize the phone numbers of five different friends or family members. Hint: The recommended method for doing this is discussed in chapter 5, which introduces the phonetic alphabet system.

I hope you have had success completing the exercises and challenges provided here. For those of you "go-getters" who are so inclined, I've provided some additional sections with advanced challenges to aid you in getting in even more practice. Enjoy!

ADVANCED CHALLENGE: THE UNITED STATES

If you were able to complete the tasks in the previous chapter, then you are now ready to tackle some advanced challenges and take your memory skills to an even higher level. The challenge covered in this chapter will take some time to complete, but it is a great way to practice some of the core principles covered in this book. You are about to memorize all the states of the United States in alphabetical order, along with each state's capital!

Since we know that there are fifty states, the first step is to come up with either one journey that consists of fifty locations, or two journeys that consist of twenty-five locations each. It doesn't matter which option you choose. I personally prefer to keep my journeys smaller and have more of them, but it's important to experiment and find out what works best for you. The journey method has been covered in detail in previous chapters, so you should be clear on how to create your journey or set of journeys at this point. Review the fifty locations of your journey(s) and make sure that you can recite them all from memory before proceeding to the next paragraph.

Now that you have your journey(s) ready to go, I'd like you to review a list of all the states in alphabetical order. Do not attempt to memorize them at this point. Simply familiarize yourself with the list of states by reviewing it a few times before proceeding to the next step.

Here's the list:

Alabama	**Montana**
Alaska	**Nebraska**
Arizona	**Nevada**
Arkansas	**New Hampshire**
California	**New Jersey**
Colorado	**New Mexico**
Connecticut	**New York**
Delaware	**North Carolina**
Florida	**North Dakota**
Georgia	**Ohio**
Hawaii	**Oklahoma**
Idaho	**Oregon**
Illinois	**Pennsylvania**
Indiana	**Rhode Island**
Iowa	**South Carolina**
Kansas	**South Dakota**
Kentucky	**Tennessee**
Louisiana	**Texas**
Maine	**Utah**
Maryland	**Vermont**
Massachusetts	**Virginia**
Michigan	**Washington**
Minnesota	**West Virginia**
Mississippi	**Wisconsin**
Missouri	**Wyoming**

Now that you've reviewed the state list, it's time to memorize the states in alphabetical order. To pull this off, you'll merely need to come up with an image to remind you of each state and mentally link the imagery to the locations of your journey. As I mentioned earlier in the book, the imagery that you come up with does not need to perfectly match the information you are trying to remember. It simply has to remind you in some way of the information. This will become even clearer as we progress with this challenge. If, at any point in this chapter, you find that I'm describing a person, place, or thing with which you're unfamiliar, please feel free to do a quick web search.

At the first location of your journey, picture Bamm-Bamm from *The Flintstones* animated series. This will be enough to remind you of **Alabama**. For now, just see Bamm-Bamm as vividly as you can. We'll add more action to the imagery later when we cover each state's capital. I'm covering the capitals separately so that you can rattle off all the states, even if you decide not to master the capitals later on.

At the following location of your journey, you see Al (Sharpton) asking a question. This imagery of *Al asking* will call to mind **Alaska**.

Next up, you see a razor. Picture a gigantic razor to make it more memorable. *A razor* will remind you of **Arizona**.

At the subsequent location, you see a giant ark. Think of Noah's Ark to help you visualize this. The ark has a large saw wedged into it. This *ark with a saw* will easily make **Arkansas** spring to mind.

A bunch of cauliflower appears at your next location. It's scattered all over your journey's location. This imagery of *cauliflower* should be enough to remind you of **California**.

At the next stop in your journey, you see a large and brightly colored shirt collar sticking out of the location. This imagery of the strange *collar* will prompt you think of **Colorado**.

At the next location of your journey, a large version of the popular game Connect Four® appears. Be sure to focus on *Connect*. This imagery of *Connect* Four will be enough to remind you of **Connecticut**.

Next up is a giant Dell® computer. Seeing a *Dell* there will conjure up the name **Delaware**.

At the next location of your journey, you see piles and piles of fluoride toothpaste. *Fluoride* will easily remind you of **Florida**.

At the following location, you encounter Curious George. Curious *George* will make you think of **Georgia**.

A beautiful Hawaiian luau is in progress at your next location. This *Hawaiian* luau will remind you of **Hawaii**.

Next on your route, you see a giant Idaho potato. The *Idaho* potato will immediately call to mind **Idaho**.

At the next location of your journey is someone who looks quite ill. The *ill*-looking person will remind you of **Illinois**.

Indiana Jones appears at the subsequent location on your journey. Seeing *Indiana* Jones will easily conjure up the name **Indiana**.

At the next location of your journey is a gigantic eye. This gigantic *eye* will cue up the memory of **Iowa**.

Next up on your journey you see a large pile of tin cans. These tin *cans* will remind you of **Kansas**.

Tasty buckets of Kentucky Fried Chicken (KFC) grace your next location. The *Kentucky* Fried Chicken will call to mind **Kentucky**.

At the next stop on your journey, you see packages of Louis Rich™ turkey breast. *Louis* Rich will help remind you of **Louisiana**.

A horse with a long, flowing mane gallops across your next location. Be sure to focus on the mane, rather than the horse. This horse's *mane* will call to mind **Maine**.

Posing at the next location of your journey is Marilyn Monroe. This famous *Marilyn* will remind you of **Maryland**.

At the subsequent location, you see a guy who, for some strange reason, is chewing on a bunch of seats. Think of this imagery as *chew seats* to remind you of **Massachusetts**.

A large machine gun appears at the following location. The sound of the word *machine gun* will make you think of **Michigan**.

At the next location of your journey, you see a miniature can of soda spinning. This *mini soda* will call to mind **Minnesota**.

Next up on your journey is Mrs. Doubtfire. This famous *Mrs.* recalls **Mississippi**.

At the next location of your journey, you see Kathy Bates as she looked in the movie *Misery*. Thinking of this *Misery* will effectively remind you of **Missouri**.

So far, you've gone through the first twenty-five locations of your journey (or journeys). I'd like you now to review the images you've placed at the first twenty-five locations. I encourage you to reread the paragraphs above that describe the imagery while doing your mental review. Review the images a few times before proceeding to the following paragraphs, which will tackle the last twenty-five locations and corresponding images.

Proceeding to the next location on your journey, a gigantic mountain rises from the earth. Seeing this *mountain* will remind you of **Montana**.

A large and shiny brass object with a cut in it shows up at the next location. Thinking of it as *brass cut* will make you recall **Nebraska**.

A bunch of slot machines appear at your next location. Envision these *slot machines in Las Vegas* to remind you of the state of **Nevada**.

Next on your journey's route you come across a large, overflowing clothes hamper. This *hamper* will call to mind **New Hampshire**.

The next location of your journey is covered by a brand-new sports jersey. This *new sports jersey* will easily remind you of **New Jersey**.

Next on your mental journey, visualize a new restaurant serving Mexican cuisine. This *new Mexican restaurant* will conjure up **New Mexico**.

At the next location of your journey, a big apple is rolling around. This *big apple* will easily make you think of **New York**.

For some strange reason, the next location looks like it's located at the North Pole! A group of people sing Christmas carols there. Christmas *carols in the North* will remind you of **North Carolina**.

The next location of your journey also looks like it's at the North Pole, but here you see a series of strange symbols in the snow that you try to decode. Trying to *decode in the North* will call to mind **North Dakota**.

Next up on your journey, a large letter *O* appears high up in the air. This *high O* will remind you of **Ohio**.

At the next location of your journey, you come across a home made of okra. This *okra home* will call to mind **Oklahoma**.

A large gun completely covered with Oreo® cookies appears at your next location. This *Oreo gun* will easily remind you of **Oregon**.

At the next location of your journey is a giant pencil. This *pencil* will make you think of **Pennsylvania**.

You are amazed to discover a red-colored island at the next stop on your journey. Seeing this *red island* will remind you of **Rhode Island**.

Next up on your journey are people singing Christmas carols. You notice that they hold compasses with arrows pointing south. Think of these people as *south carolers* and you'll be reminded of **South Carolina**.

The next location of your journey is covered in south-pointing compasses. You notice strange symbols all over the compasses and attempt to decode them. When visualizing this, focus on *south* and *decode* to make **South Dakota** spring to mind.

Someone is playing tennis at the next stop on your journey. This image of *tennis* will call to mind **Tennessee**.

The next location of your journey is completely covered in Texas toast. This *Texas toast* will naturally remind you of **Texas**.

An amazing performance by the Mormon Tabernacle Choir is in progress at your next location. The *Mormon Tabernacle Choir* should conjure up the state of **Utah**.

At the next location of your journey, a group of vermin runs around. Seeing the *vermin* should remind you of **Vermont**.

A large statue of the Virgin Mary appears at the next stop on your journey. This famous *Virgin* makes you think of **Virginia**.

At the next location of your journey, you see a giant washing machine. This *washing machine* will remind you of **Washington**.

Next up, a Virgin America airplane flies west through your subsequent location. This *westbound Virgin* plane should conjure up the state of **West Virginia**.

A giant bottle of whiskey appears at the next location. Seeing this *whiskey* should be enough to make you think of **Wisconsin**.

At the last location of your journey, you see a large letter *Y* with a homing pigeon flying around it. Think of this as *Y homing* and you'll easily be reminded of **Wyoming**.

Now, mentally review all of the images at your fifty locations. Do this three times, rereading the paragraphs above as necessary. Remember to have fun and approach this more as an exercise in using your creativity and imagination than as a difficult or boring memory exercise.

You can now recite all of the U.S. states in alphabetical order! Are you ready to take this advanced challenge to the next level? You will now add to the imagery at your fifty locations, so you will also be able to remember every state's capital. You can do this! If you were able to complete the first part of the challenge, this last part will be easy for you.

As we did with the states, I'd first like you to familiarize yourself with the list of capital cities before you begin to memorize them. Since you are probably not quite as familiar with the names of the capital cities as you are with the names of the states, spend a little extra time with this list. Read through the list five times to become familiar with each city's name. You are not memorizing anything at this point, but simply familiarizing yourself with the list. This will help you to connect more easily with the imagery I describe later on.

Here is the list:

Montgomery	Helena
Juneau	Lincoln
Phoenix	Carson City
Little Rock	Concord
Sacramento	Trenton
Denver	Santa Fe
Hartford	Albany
Dover	Raleigh
Tallahassee	Bismarck
Atlanta	Columbus
Honolulu	Oklahoma City
Boise	Salem
Springfield	Harrisburg
Indianapolis	Providence
Des Moines	Columbia
Topeka	Pierre
Frankfort	Nashville
Baton Rouge	Austin
Augusta	Salt Lake City
Annapolis	Montpelier
Boston	Richmond
Lansing	Olympia
St. Paul	Charleston
Jackson	Madison
Jefferson City	Cheyenne

Now that you've reviewed the list of capital cities, it's time to memorize them and connect them to their corresponding states. To accomplish this, you'll simply need to come up with imagery to remind you of each capital city, and then link that imagery to the existing state imagery at the various locations of your journey.

Basically, you'll just be adding to the imagery already at the fifty journey locations for the states. Again, it's important to note that the imagery you add merely needs to remind you of the capital city's name in some way. We are now going to revisit all fifty of your journey locations and adjust the imagery so that it reminds you of both the state and its capital city.

At the first location of your journey, Bamm-Bamm (Alabama) from *The Flintstones* animated TV series is romping around. Bamm-Bamm starts to chew on a huge mountain of gum and blow bubbles. This *mountain of gum* will make you think of **Montgomery**.

We simply adjusted and added to the imagery so that it now reminds you of both the state and its capital. This is easy and fun! Let's continue.

Next up, you have *Al asking* (Alaska). After Al finishes asking, he then starts to repeatedly circle the month of June on a calendar. The circle gets darker and darker around the month of June and it starts to look like an *O*. Think of this as *June O* and you'll be reminded of **Juneau**.

At the following location, you see *a razor* (Arizona). This razor starts to shave off the feathers of a fiery phoenix! Visualizing this fiery *phoenix* should naturally conjure up **Phoenix**.

Next up, an *ark with a saw* (Arkansas) appears. Suddenly a little rock shoots out of the ark! This keeps happening over and over again. One little rock after another shoots out of the ark. Seeing each *little rock* will call to mind **Little Rock**.

At the subsequent location on your journey, a bunch of *cauliflower* (California) springs up. The cauliflower magically starts to hop into a large sack all by itself. This *sack* should be enough to remind you of **Sacramento**.

A strange *collar* (Colorado) appears next on your journey. The collar starts to multiply into hundreds of collars that then fill up a dragon's den. Visualize that happening to the dragon's *den* and you'll be reminded of **Denver**.

At the next location of your journey is a large version of the game *Connect* Four (Connecticut). Suddenly, each red piece in the game magically morphs into a heart! The hearts then start to fly into the back of a Ford. Think of this as being *heart Ford* and **Hartford** will spring to mind.

At the following location, you have a giant *Dell* computer (Delaware). A dove appears out of nowhere and starts to peck on the Dell's screen, making holes in it. This imagery of the *dove* makes you think of **Dover**.

Piles and piles of *fluoride* toothpaste (Florida) accumulate at the next stop on your journey. The toothpaste starts to squirt onto a bunch of tall hats and pushes them into the sea. These *tall hats at sea* will remind you of **Tallahassee**.

At the following location, you see Curious *George* (Georgia). Curious George starts to guzzle down a giant bottle of Mylanta® antacid. *Mylanta* should call to mind **Atlanta**.

A *Hawaiian* luau (Hawaii) is going on at the next stop on your journey. Everyone at the luau starts to put on Lululemon® clothing! This imagery of *Lululemon* should remind you of **Honolulu**.

At the subsequent location on your journey is a giant *Idaho* potato (Idaho). A group of young boys start to eat the potato all at once. These *boys* will call to mind **Boise**.

Next up, you envision a person who is very *ill* (Illinois). This person starts to cough up a bunch of bouncy springs, which then begin to form a field. This *spring field* will help you recall **Springfield**.

At the next stop on your journey appears *Indiana* Jones (Indiana). Indiana Jones starts to eat giant apples with his picture on them. These *Indiana apples* will make you think of **Indianapolis**.

A gigantic *eye* (Iowa) shows up at your next stop. A lawn mower shoots out of the eye and starts mowing your journey's location. This imagery of *mowing* should remind you of **Des Moines**.

At the next location of your journey is a large pile of tin *cans* (Kansas). One of the cans magically morphs into what at first looks to you like a tin toothpick, but it then starts to pick at a giant toe. You realize that this is a *toe pick*, making you think of **Topeka**.

Tasty buckets of *Kentucky* Fried Chicken (Kentucky) are arrayed throughout the next stop on your journey. Strangely, beef franks start to shoot out of the buckets. The franks join together and they slowly form a large fort. This *frank fort* will make **Frankfort** spring to mind.

At the next location of your journey, you have turkey breast from *Louis* Rich (Louisiana). The turkey grabs a baton that has a brush on the end, and it uses this baton to apply some rouge. Think of this as being *baton rouge* and you'll instantly be reminded of the city **Baton Rouge**.

A horse with a long, flowing *mane* (Maine) trots through your next location. The mane starts to wrap itself around a giant calendar that is turned to the month of August. Focusing on *August* will call to mind **Augusta**.

The famous *Marilyn* Monroe (Maryland) poses glamorously at your next location. Marilyn starts to play with a Raggedy Ann doll. Then the doll begins to munch on some apples! Think of this imagery as *Ann apples* and you'll be reminded of **Annapolis**.

Next up, you watch a guy *chew seats* (Massachusetts). After he's done chewing the seats, this same guy starts to eat a delicious-looking Boston cream pie! This *Boston cream pie* will easily make you remember **Boston**.

At the next location of your journey, you see a large *machine gun* (Michigan). A sharp lance suddenly pierces the machine gun and starts to vibrate. This *lance* should remind you of **Lansing**.

A spinning can of *mini soda* (Minnesota) appears at your next location. You are surprised to see Saint Paul from the Bible pick up the can and start to drink it! This *Saint Paul* will call to mind the city of **St. Paul**.

At the next location of your journey you come upon Mrs. Doubtfire, a famous *Mrs.* (Mississippi). This Mrs. starts to sing and dance with the Jackson 5. Seeing the *Jackson 5* will remind you of **Jackson**.

Now you encounter Kathy Bates from the movie *Misery* (Missouri) at the next stop on your journey. This "Misery" suddenly walks into a brightly lit city. She's surprised to discover that everyone in the city looks exactly like Thomas Jefferson! Think of this place as *Jefferson City* and you'll conjure up the capital, **Jefferson City**.

At this point, you've added images for the capitals to your first twenty-five journey locations. Go ahead and review the images at these locations. You can reread the paragraphs above while doing your mental review. Be sure to review all images at least a few times before you proceed.

At the next location of your journey, a gigantic *mountain* (Montana) confronts you. Magically, a thousand ships emerge from the mountain and set sail toward Helen of Troy! This famous *Helen* should remind you of **Helena**.

Next up on your journey is the image for *brass cut* (Nebraska). Abraham Lincoln suddenly appears and starts to continuously throw the brass object in the air. This famous *Lincoln* will call to mind the capital city, **Lincoln**.

At the following location, a bunch of *slot machines in Las Vegas* (Nevada) are flashing lights. These Las Vegas slot machines start to hop toward a city. It turns out that everyone in this city looks like Ben Carson! Think of this as *Carson City* and **Carson City** will spring to mind.

A large clothes *hamper* (New Hampshire) appears at your next location. You now notice a large cord hanging out of the hamper. The cord is covered in pictures of what look like convicts. This *con cord* will remind you of **Concord**.

Next up on your journey is a *new sports jersey* (New Jersey). The jersey suddenly appears on the side of a large train. The train then smashes into a giant weight labeled 1 TON and explodes. Think of this imagery as a *train ton* and you will conjure up the name **Trenton**.

At the next location of your journey, you have a *new Mexican restaurant* (New Mexico). You notice that Santa Claus is dining in the restaurant! This famous *Santa* should remind you of **Santa Fe**.

You reach a *big apple* (New York) at the next stop on your journey. An old bunny starts to roll the apple around and play with it. This *old bunny* should remind you of **Albany**.

At the next location of your journey, you hear people singing *carols in the North* (North Carolina). Suddenly, these carolers are joined by thousands of people holding up signs to form a rally. This *rally* makes you think of **Raleigh**.

Symbols that you attempt to *decode in the North* (North Dakota) form the next stop on your journey. The symbols suddenly decode themselves and reveal a picture of a bus with a large, dark mark on it. This *bus mark* will remind you of **Bismarck**.

At the next location of your journey, you have a *high O* (Ohio). Marble columns start to shoot through the *O* and smash into a large bus. Think of this scenario as *columns bus* and **Columbus** will spring to mind.

An *okra home* (Oklahoma) appears at your next location. This home magically starts to multiply into hundreds of okra homes until an entire city is formed. This *okra home city* will remind you of **Oklahoma City**.

At your subsequent location is an *Oreo gun* (Oregon). This Oreo gun starts to shoot Oreo cookies at people watching a Salem witch trial, and cookies smash into their faces. This *Salem witch trial* will conjure up the capital, **Salem**.

A giant *pencil* (Pennsylvania) shows up at your next location. The pencil starts to write all over what at first looks like an iceberg. The iceberg, however, morphs as the pencil writes on it, growing hair all over until it's completely covered. Think of it now as a *hairs berg* and this will remind you of **Harrisburg**.

At the following location is a red-colored island or *red island* (Rhode Island). A bright-white glow starts to surround the island, forming what looks like a shield around it. You surmise that the island is now being protected by *divine providence*. This imagery should make you think of **Providence**.

A bunch of *south carolers* (South Carolina) sing their hearts out at the following location. These "south carolers" all start to climb a gigantic column that has an enormous bee perched on top. The bee then stings the carolers. This *column bee* will remind you of **Columbia**.

Next up is a scene depicting *south* and *decode* (South Dakota). After the south-pointing compasses are decoded, they hop onto a fishing pier and then jump into the water, creating huge splashes. The fishing *pier* makes **Pierre** spring to mind.

Someone plays *tennis* (Tennessee) at your next location. The tennis player's racket magically turns into a guitar and he starts to play country music. This scenario should remind you of **Nashville**, which is famous for country music.

The next location of your journey is completely covered with *Texas toast* (Texas)—which Austin Powers starts to scarf down enthusiastically. *Austin* Powers eating the Texas toast will call to mind **Austin**.

An amazing performance by the *Mormon Tabernacle Choir* (Utah) rings out at your next location. Members of the choir start to jump into the Great Salt Lake. (If it helps, you can visualize salt shakers floating in the lake.) The image of the *Great Salt Lake* will remind you of **Salt Lake City**.

At the next location of your journey is a bunch of *vermin* (Vermont). One of the vermin grows to be the size of Godzilla, and somehow manages to peel off the top of a mountain. This *mountain peeler* will make you think of **Montpelier**.

A large statue of the *Virgin* Mary (Virginia) graces your next location. You push the statue up a mountain that has incredible riches at its peak. This *rich mountain* should remind you of **Richmond**.

At the following location is a giant *washing machine* (Washington). Olympic athletes start to come out of the washing machine one by one as part of the opening ceremony of the Olympics. This imagery of the *Olympics* will make **Olympia** spring to mind.

The *westbound Virgin* plane (West Virginia) appears at your next location. This plane crashes into a giant billboard of Prince Charles, made of tin. Think of this billboard as being *Charles tin* and you'll be reminded of **Charleston**.

At the subsequent location is a giant bottle of *whiskey* (Wisconsin). The actress Virginia Madsen drinks the entire bottle! This famous *Madsen* will make you think of **Madison**.

Last up on your journey is a large letter *Y* with a homing pigeon flying around it, representing *Y homing* (Wyoming). The Y and the homing pigeon start to fly around the actress *Anne* Hathaway, who does her best to *shy* away from them. Think of *shy Anne* when you want to remember **Cheyenne**.

Now, once again mentally review all the images at your fifty locations. Do this five times, rereading the paragraphs above as necessary. As we did earlier, remember to have fun and approach this as a creative exercise, rather than a memory chore. That unique approach is important to your continued success in developing your memory skills.

Congratulations! You can now recite all the states in the United States in alphabetical order, as well as their capitals! This is an impressive feat of memory. In the next section, we'll take these skills "across the pond" and practice these techniques with European countries.

ADVANCED CHALLENGE: EUROPE

If you completed the previous advanced challenge of
memorizing all U.S. states in alphabetical order, along with their
capitals, you should be able to complete this challenge as well,
although it may be a bit more difficult—after all, that's why it's an
advanced challenge. You are about to memorize the names of all
the countries of Europe in alphabetical order!

There are fifty different countries in Europe (as we go to print,
that is—you never know!), so the first step, as was the case for the
U.S. challenge, is to come up with either one journey that consists
of fifty locations, or two journeys of twenty-five locations each.
Again, it doesn't matter which you choose. At this point, you should
have enough experience with the journey method to decide what
works best for you. Be sure to review the fifty locations of your
journey(s) and make sure you can recite them all from memory
before proceeding to the next paragraph.

Now that you have your journey(s) ready to go, it's time to review the list of European countries in alphabetical order. Do not attempt to memorize them at this point. You simply need to familiarize yourself with the list of countries first. Reviewing this list a few times will make it easier for you to make a connection later between the imagery I describe and the name of each corresponding country.

Here is the list:

Albania	**Liechtenstein**
Andorra	**Lithuania**
Armenia	**Luxembourg**
Austria	**Macedonia**
Azerbaijan	**Malta**
Belarus	**Moldova**
Belgium	**Monaco**
Bosnia and Herzegovina	**Montenegro**
Bulgaria	**Netherlands**
Croatia	**Norway**
Cyprus	**Poland**
Czech Republic	**Portugal**
Denmark	**Romania**
Estonia	**Russia**
Finland	**San Marino**
France	**Serbia**
Georgia	**Slovakia**
Germany	**Slovenia**
Greece	**Spain**
Hungary	**Sweden**
Iceland	**Switzerland**
Ireland	**Turkey**
Italy	**Ukraine**
Kazakhstan	**United Kingdom**
Latvia	**Vatican City**

Now that you've reviewed the list of countries, it's time to memorize them. To accomplish this, we'll follow the same process as we did with the U.S. states and capitals. I'll describe some imagery that should remind you of each country's name and you'll simply visualize it all happening at the corresponding location of your journey. Again, if at any point in this chapter, you find that I'm describing a person, place, or thing with which you're unfamiliar, please feel free to do a quick web search. Let's begin!

First off on your journey, you see Al Pacino spin around and suddenly turn into the comic book super-villain Bane. Think of this image as *Al Bane* to remind you of **Albania**.

At the next location of your journey, you see a giant ant attack Dora the Explorer. Think of this scenario as being *ant Dora* and you'll think of **Andorra**.

Next up on your journey you see Kim Kardashian leading an army in a dance. The *army* will give you one way to remember **Armenia**. Since Kim Kardashian is a famous person of *Armenian* descent, that's a second reminder.

At the next location of your journey, you see Arnold Schwarzenegger posing as a bodybuilder. This famous actor of *Austrian* descent should remind you of **Austria**.

A gigantic eraser is magically erasing a Best Buy® building at the following location. Once the building has been erased, you see John Lennon, who was apparently the only one in the building. Think of this crazy scenario as *eraser Buy John* and it will call to mind **Azerbaijan**.

At the next location of your journey, you see Belle from *Beauty and the Beast* dancing and singing. Unfortunately, her dress starts to rust! Think of *Belle rust* to remind you of **Belarus**.

A bunch of delicious-looking Belgian waffles appear at your next location. Go ahead and imagine eating them. These *Belgian waffles* should easily call to mind **Belgium**.

Next up, you see your boss hit his knee and then jump into

a hearse. Strangely, this hearse then starts to go up a giant vine. Think of this scenario as being *boss knee hearse go vine* and **Bosnia and Herzegovina** will spring to mind.

At the next location of your journey, a burglar is stealing something. This image of a *burglar* should be enough to remind you of **Bulgaria**.

A giant crow pecks and caws at the following location. This *crow* should make you think of **Croatia**.

At the next location on your journey, a large cypress tree keeps growing taller and changing colors. This *cypress* tree will remind you of **Cyprus**.

A giant cashier's check spins and spins at your subsequent location. This cashier's *check* will make you think of the **Czech Republic**.

The next location of your journey has a large dent in it. This dent becomes stained with a big black mark. Visualize this *dent mark* and **Denmark** will spring to mind.

At the next location of your journey, you see a gigantic stone. This stone magically starts to morph into the shape of an S. This *S stone* will call to mind **Estonia**.

A large fin appears at the next stop on your journey. This fin flies around for a while and then lands. It does this over and over again. Think of *fin land* and you'll be reminded of **Finland**.

At the following location, the Eiffel Tower rises toward the sky. The *Eiffel Tower* should easily make you think of **France**.

Next up, you see Curious George monkeying around. This image of *Curious George* should remind you of **Georgia**.

At your subsequent location, the Berlin Wall is crumbling. This image of the *Berlin Wall* should call to mind **Germany**.

The next stop on your journey is completely covered with grease. There is grease everywhere! This image of *grease* will remind you of **Greece**.

At the next location, you see all your favorite foods. This luscious array of food makes you incredibly hungry. Focus on feeling *hungry* when you visualize this location of your journey, and you'll think of **Hungary**.

Giant ice cubes are everywhere at your next location. Seeing all this *ice* will remind you of **Iceland**.

At the following location, you see a leprechaun jumping into a pot of gold! This *leprechaun* will conjure up an image of **Ireland**.

The famous Leaning Tower of Pisa appears at your next location, and it has a giant bowl of pasta on top of it. These images of the *Leaning Tower of Pisa* and *pasta* should remind you of **Italy**.

At the next location of your journey, a car drives into a giant sock. This causes the sock to develop an ugly stain. Visualize this happening a few times. *Car sock stain* will help you call to mind **Kazakhstan**.

You see and smell a nice cup of latte at the following location. As you drink the latte, you see a brightly colored V form in the middle of it. Think of *latte V* to remember **Latvia**.

You've made it through the first twenty-five locations! Review the images at these locations a few times before proceeding to the following paragraphs, which will tackle the last twenty-five locations and corresponding images. Feel free to reread the paragraphs above while doing your review.

At the next location of your journey, a giant tongue starts to lick Frankenstein! Call him "Stein" for short. Think of *licking Stein* and **Liechtenstein** will spring to mind.

The famous actor John Lithgow appears at the subsequent location, drinking a glass of wine. Think of this as being *Lithgow wine* and you'll be reminded of **Lithuania**.

At the following location of your journey, a giant iceberg is covered in gold, diamonds, and other jewels that make it look incredibly luxe. This *luxe berg* will conjure up the name **Luxembourg**.

A massive doughnut is spinning around at the next stop on your journey. This *massive doughnut* will remind you of **Macedonia**.

A delicious-looking chocolate malt appears at your next

location. You start to drink the malt and are amazed at how good it tastes! This *malt* will make you think of **Malta**.

At the next location of your journey, you see green mold growing high in the air. The mold keeps growing until it eventually folds over. Think of *mold over* and **Moldova** will come to mind.

Monica from the TV show *Friends* does jumping jacks while singing the *Friends* theme song at your next location. Visualizing *Monica* will help remind you of **Monaco**.

Next up, you see a large mountain. At the top of the mountain, a delicious-looking giant egg roll appears! Think of this *mountain egg roll* to remember **Montenegro**.

The next location of your journey is very dark, and you see a bunch of ghosts and goblins flying around. Think of this location as the *nether realm* and you'll be reminded of the **Netherlands**.

You next encounter on your journey a large doorway with a sign above it that says NO WAY. Curious, you try to get past the doorway, but some magical force stops you. No matter what you try, there's just "no way" to get through. This scenario with *no way* will bring to mind **Norway**.

At the next location of your journey, a large firefighter's pole appears. For fun, you decide to climb up and then slide down the pole. This *pole* will remind you of **Poland**.

A nice bottle of port wine awaits you at your next location. Just as you are about to drink it, a gull swoops in and flies away with the bottle! Think of this *port gull* and **Portugal** will spring to mind.

Next up on your journey, Dracula is biting into some Romaine lettuce! The *Romaine* lettuce will give you one way to remember **Romania**. Also, since *Dracula* is a famous fictional character from Transylvania, which is part of Romania, visualizing him will trigger another reminder.

Vladimir Putin is flexing his muscles at the following location on your journey. This image of *Vladimir Putin* should easily remind you of **Russia**.

Next up on your journey, the famous quarterback Dan Marino is throwing a football around. He suddenly yells at you, "Hi! My name is Dan Marino and I'm from San Marino." This strange scenario with *Dan Marino* will conjure up the name **San Marino**.

At the following location, Sir Lancelot is attacking a giant killer bee. Think of *Sir bee* to remind you of **Serbia**.

A vacuum cleaner moves slowly, vacuuming things up at your next location. This image of a *slow vac* should make you think of **Slovakia**.

A large vine appears at the subsequent location on your journey. This vine wraps itself around your location, moving incredibly slowly. With this image of a *slow vine*, **Slovenia** should spring to mind.

At the next location of your journey, a Spanish bullfighter is dodging a charging bull. This *Spanish bullfighter* will help remind you of **Spain**.

A delicious bowl of Swedish meatballs appears at the following location. Go ahead and imagine eating them. These *Swedish meatballs* will make you think of **Sweden**.

Next up on your journey is a giant block of Swiss cheese. You climb up the block of cheese, eating some along the way. This *Swiss cheese* will naturally remind you of **Switzerland**.

At the next location of your journey, a large, tasty-looking Thanksgiving turkey graces a large table. This Thanksgiving *turkey* will call to mind the nation of **Turkey**.

A U-shaped crane continuously lifts and drops some large crates at the subsequent location on your journey. This *U-crane* will remind you of **Ukraine**.

Next up on your journey, a United Airlines plane is flying above what looks like a magical kingdom. When the plane lands, you see United Airlines planes everywhere. Think of this place as being a *United kingdom* and the **United Kingdom** will spring to mind.

At the last location of your journey, you see the pope blessing people. This image of the *pope* should call to mind **Vatican City**.

Mentally review the images at your fifty journey locations. Do this five times, rereading the paragraphs above as necessary. As always, remember to approach this as a fun and creative exercise. Ideally, you will be smiling as you visualize each scenario happening at the various locations.

Congratulations! You have completed an amazing challenge and can now name all the countries in Europe alphabetically. You might just be ready to become the next USA National Memory Champion!

ACKNOWLEDGMENTS

I'd like to express my sincere thanks and appreciation to my mother, Roxanne, for all she's done for me throughout my life; to my friend and business mentor Mike Faith for all of his help and valuable advice over the years; to my friend and client Cash Nickerson for inspiring me with his success in so many areas; to my friend Harry Villegas for his years of moral support and for being a great sounding board; to my friend and client Ron Mallia for inspiring me with his business acumen and achievements; to JB Lorda for all of his help and support over the years; to my personal trainer Giana Lando for helping to keep my body in shape while I work my mind; to all of my many friends and tennis partners at the San Francisco Tennis Club who have in many ways supported my various endeavors for the past two decades; to Alex McIntyre, Marissa Dagdagan, Amanda Tong, Mark Lee, Dennis Wong, David Rumbaugh, Tomas Venegas, Tony Romero, Savan Devani, and all of my other friends from school who put up with the vivid imagination that helped me become a memory champion; to the incredible Ed Addeo for all of his invaluable help getting this book out; to my amazing literary agent, Bob Diforio, for his help with my various works; and to the incredibly talented team at Sterling Publishing for all of their superb work and for believing in this book.

INDEX

ABOUT THE AUTHOR

Chester Santos, "The International Man of Memory,"™ has left
an impression on all corners of the earth. Through his ability to
demonstrate extraordinary feats of the mind, as well as educate
others to do the same, this U.S. Memory Champion is widely
regarded to be one of the greatest memory experts in the
world. He has helped thousands of people to realize the benefits
of an improved memory and sharper mind, and has appeared in
the *New York Times, Wall Street Journal, San Francisco Chronicle,
Washington Post, USA Today,* PBS, CNN, and various other
television, radio, and print media all over the world. Through
workshops, corporate training seminars, and his world-renowned
speeches and presentations, Santos has developed a knack for
passing on valuable memory techniques in ways that are easy to
understand and retain for years to come. He has been a speaker
for executive organizations such as YPO, CEO Clubs International,
and AceTech, as well as for many Fortune 500 companies,
and prestigious universities including the Royal University for
Women in Bahrain, the Haas Graduate School of Business
in Berkeley, Stanford University, and Harvard University.